SCENTED GIFTS

SCENTED GIFTS

JANE NEWDICK

Photographs by Di Lewis

a Salamander book

Published by Salamander Books Limited
LONDON

A SALAMANDER BOOK

Published by Salamander Books Ltd
129-137 York Way
London N7 9LG
United Kingdom

ISBN: 0-517-12154-9

Distributed by Random House Value Publishing, Inc.,
40 Engelhard Avenue, Avenel, New Jersey 07001

A CIP catalog record for this book is available from the Library of Congress

1   3   5   7   9   8   6   4   2

All correspondence concerning the content of this volume should be
addressed to Salamander Books Ltd.

COMMISSIONING EDITOR
Lisa Dyer

PHOTOGRAPHER
Di Lewis

DESIGN
Bridgewater Book Company/Ron Bryant-Funnell

COLOR SEPARATION
P&W Graphics Pte Ltd, Singapore

Printed in Italy

CONTENTS

INTRODUCTION

Scented gifts make wonderful presents, whether they are flowers, perfumes, delicious foods or decorations for the home, and have one wonderful attribute in common – their fabulous aromas. All the projects in this book are naturally scented by using dried and fresh herbs and flowers, as well as spices, fruits and essential oils, which are available in a wide variety of natural scents. Every season of the year has its own special scents, from the first hyacinths and primroses of spring through the lilies, pinks, sweet peas and roses of the summer months. Later there are the warm and rich fragrances of autumn and winter, such as pine branches, evergreens, winter fruits and spices. Apart from these well-known natural scenting agents, there are artificial fragrances, some of which capture the natural ingredient almost exactly. However, for creating just a few things at home, it is easier and more authentic to use natural scenting agents whenever possible.

Many of the projects and ideas throughout the book can be given for special occasions, such as birthdays, anniversaries, weddings, or as thank-you or welcome-home gifts. There are intimate gifts, which can be adapted to the personality of the recipient, as well as more general gifts. Ideas for presenting your gifts in scented and stylish ways are included in the last chapter of the book.

Flower and Herb Scents

A fabulous profusion of flowers to buy, both dried and fresh, is available all year round, and you may have a garden which can provide your own select types of flowers. Even florists' flowers, after years of looking beautiful but having no scent, are finally being bred to recapture the proper fragrances we expect. Fresh herbs, too, are available throughout the year, and even dried herbs have enough scent to use them in both culinary and decorative projects. Some fragrant flowers, such as lavender and roses, have both decorative and herbal qualities, which makes them endlessly versatile.

Drying Flowers and Herbs

Many of the projects on the following pages require dried herbs and flowers, which can be bought or dried yourself. Although some scent is lost in the drying process, certain flowers and herbs are excellent at keeping their scent, such as rose and lavender, and most herbs, especially those from silver-leaved and woody-stemmed varieties, such as thyme, artemesias and marjoram, also keep their scent well. Boosting the scent of dried flowers and herbs can be achieved with the addition of a little essential oil in the same scent. Also, using fixatives such as orris root powder in dried flower mixtures helps to hold the fragrance.

Air drying is the easiest method of drying herbs and flowers at home. The most suitable flowers and herbs for drying include: roses, lavender, jasmine, orange blossom, chamomile, elder, marigold, lemon verbena, eucalyptus, marjoram, sage, meadowsweet, rosemary, artemesia, thyme, basil, sweet geranium and mint. Flowers should be picked when they are just fully opened, and on a dry day in the late

RIGHT Scented gifts look best when prettily presented with fresh flowers, or you could decorate the gift with some of the natural ingredients used in the project.

morning when their volatile oils are at their peak. Pick herbs for drying when the leaves are a good size, but still fresh and young, again on a sunny day if possible.

The easiest drying method is to gather the herbs or flowers into loose bunches and tie with rubber bands, although larger flower spikes are best left to dry singly. Hang the bunches securely with pliable garden wire or twine in a warm, dark and dry place with good air circulation. The best places are high in a dry outbuilding, in an airing cupboard or above a kitchen range which is permanently on. However, you must ensure that the area remains moisture-free. Small flower heads or petals are best dried between layers of fine mesh screen in a dark, dry and warm area. After the flowers and herbs are dry, you can pick the petals and leaves, or keep them whole, depending on how you will be using them.

Spice and Fruit Scents
~

In addition to herbs and flowers, spices have wonderful scents and flavours. Although many spices are indigenous to just a small part of the world, some, such as pepper, cinnamon, vanilla and ginger, have become widespread, appearing commonly in household kitchens. Beyond the culinary sphere, spices can be used to scent a variety of decorative and practical objects.

Fragrances can also be captured from fruits, and the most useful and outstanding fruits are those from the citrus family, such as limes, lemons, oranges and grapefruit. The dried peel from these fruits can be used to bring a citrus scent to pot-pourris, foods and decorations for the home. The oils in the skins of these fruits are also distilled to create powerfully scented essential oils.

Essential Oils
~

The uses of plant and flower essential oils are becoming more fully recognised year by year, and their availability has increased dramatically. Purely natural, the oils are the essence of the plant's perfume, and obtained from the petals, leaves, bark and seeds of the plant. They should not be confused with 'aromatherapy oils' which are blends,

BELOW LEFT AND RIGHT
Both fresh and dried natural materials, ranging from delicious spices to delicate flowers, are the basic ingredients for many scented gifts.

sometimes with chemicals added. Generally the oils are true to the plants or fruit from which they are derived, so that cinnamon oil smells of cinnamon and orange oil of orange, for example. The oils can be used to provide scent in food, perfumes, cosmetics and decorations. They are highly concentrated and must be used with care, but can be the source of wonderfully creative gifts.

Because essential oils may cause skin irritation in their concentrated form, they are used in tiny amounts and almost always diluted. Care should be taken when handling the oils and never apply them directly to the skin. They should always be used with a dropper, which enables measuring the oil drop by drop and eliminates direct contact with the skin. Always read carefully the information that is included with the essential oils.

Some essential oils are not suitable for women who are pregnant; these include pennyroyal, sage, oregano, basil, hyssop, juniper, myrrh, fennel, rosemary and clary sage. Also, some oils should not be used for sensitive skins, such as thyme, basil, lemon, lemongrass, peppermint, tea-tree or pine. Fennel, hyssop and sage should not be used in products for people with epilepsy. If in doubt, consult additional information on essential oils.

Essential oils should be stored upright in a cool, dark place and out of reach of children and pets. They should be kept in their dark glass bottles and never stored in plastic bottles. They will keep up to a year if properly stored, however lime, lemon and orange oils will not keep as long and should be regularly checked. Essential oils are available from health and wholefood shops and specialist herbalists. However, nowadays many other shops, such as chemists, craft shops and gift shops, also stock essential oils. Some of the most popular essential oils are described in the glossary on page 94.

ORNAMENTAL DECORATIONS

Creating decorative gifts which are scented offers a great opportunity to be ingenious and adventurous with the materials used. You can customise the gift quite carefully to cater to the personality of the gift's recipient. Choosing correct colour shades and styles to match the home where the gift will be placed shows a thoughtful approach to making presents for others. If you know that the person to whom you are giving the present is an old-fashioned romantic at heart, you can go wild with floral materials, such as roses; or, if they adore subtle and soft shades, you can choose natural-toned materials.

The trick in making home-made gifts look attractive is to take trouble with the details. Spend some time finding exactly the right width and colour of ribbon or really high-quality ingredients, such as dried flowers with almost-fresh colours. Do not embark on a new or difficult skill until you have time to perfect a simple project first. Keep the fragrances subtle but evident, and always include extra fragrance in the form of essential oils or spray scents if the gift's fragrance will need to be refreshed. Include a label with written instructions on how to add extra fragrance and when to do so, if needed, and wrap the finished gift with panache.

Dried Oranges and Lemons

Dried oranges and lemons, some gilded and others with their rinds cut into interesting patterns, look wonderful displayed in a wire-work basket or shallow bowl. You could also tie them individually with gold ribbon bows, pinning to secure, and use them as Christmas tree decorations.

SMALL FRESH UNWAXED ORANGES AND LEMONS
~
CANELLE KNIFE
~
KITCHEN KNIFE
~
THIN WIRE OR STRING
~
BRONZE POWDER AND BRONZE POWDER MEDIUM
OR GOLD GILDING CREAM,
AVAILABLE FROM ARTISTS' SUPPLY SHOPS
~
BRUSH OR SPONGE
~
DUTCH GOLD LEAF, OPTIONAL
~
SPRAY ADHESIVE, OPTIONAL

Use fruits which have not been sprayed and treated with coating waxes; look for organic and unwaxed citrus.

Leave some of the whole fruits uncut, but on others cut vertical or horizontal rings and wavy patterns with the canelle knife. This special tool cuts a narrow groove into the rind, removing a long twist of peel. Dry the whole fruits in a place where they can remain to dry completely, perhaps as long as several weeks. Ideally, there should be a circulation of warm air, such as above a ducted radiator or near a cooking range which is permanently on. Turn the fruits often, and check that they are not deteriorating. A few may not dry successfully, so discard them.

You may also like to slice some fruits into rings and thread them on to wire or string to dry, or place them one-layer-deep on a baking rack in a very low oven until dried.

Once the fruits are dried, gild them by mixing the bronze powder with the medium; the mediums can be oil-, acrylic- or cellulose-based. Brush or sponge a tiny amount of the bronze paint over the surface. Gold creams can be rubbed on to the fruit with a finger or cloth.

You may like to experiment with Dutch gold leaf, which produces a flamboyant effect.

RIGHT The burnished colours of dried and gilded citrus fruits create a stunning scented arrangement in a wire basket.

Papier-mâché Balls
~

These scented balls are fun to make, but a little messy. You can choose the colours according to the tissue paper you use. Shown here are a few balls in one colour of tissue and others combining two colours. Make a range of sizes to pile together in a bowl or spread out in a shallow tray or basket. Small balls can be strung like beads on to coloured cord or string.

OLD NEWSPAPERS OR A PLASTIC SHEET
~
CELLULOSE WALLPAPER ADHESIVE
~
BLUE AND GREEN TISSUE PAPER
~
GLUE BRUSH
~
COTTON, PAPER OR POLYSTYRENE BALL SHAPES
~
FLORAL-SCENTED ESSENTIAL OILS

BELOW Make papier-mâché balls in various sizes, rather than all one size, for a more interesting collection.

Clear a large space in which to work and cover a surface with newspapers or a plastic sheet. If the papier-mâché paste accidentally gets on the surface, wipe it off before it sets.

Mix the wallpaper paste according to the instructions on the packet. Then tear narrow strips of tissue paper from several sheets. You will find it easiest to tear in one direction, depending on how the paper grain runs. The strips can be of any length, and uneven edges are better than straight ones. Once you have a good pile of paper strips, start applying them to the balls. Either brush the paste on to the ball or on to the tissue, whichever you find easiest. Use plenty of paste and let it cover all the surfaces.

Using the brush or your fingers, press the paper down over the ball shape as you wrap the tissues strips round. Work in several directions, rather like winding string back into a ball, until you have covered the entire ball and the tissue papers are at least two to three layers thick. The tissue is really just a surface decoration and you are not attempting to build a structure as in true papier-mâché.

ABOVE Two-tone and single-colour balls make a bright display in a bowl painted to match one of the colours. Choose colours that complement the room where the balls will be displayed.

Now leave the ball in a warm, airy place to dry completely. Stand each ball on a little piece of clean tissue, so if the ball sticks you can simply tear way the excess tissue later without marking the ball.

If you prefer to add many layers of tissue paper to the ball, do so after each layer is completely dry. You may like to add a few drops of essential oil, stage by stage, after each layer has been glued and dried. Otherwise wait until the balls are completely dry, and apply about six drops of essential oil to each ball, letting the oil soak in completely. Include some extra essential oil with the balls when giving them as presents, so the scent can be refreshed.

Spice and Nut Ring

*The nuts, fruits and seed pods used in this decorative ring
create a colouring of subtle burnished brown, rich chestnut
and pale beige. You can use any decorative ingredients that
are fairly robust and completely dry. Instead of the more usual
ribbon bow, hang this ring from a rich velvet cord.*

GLUE GUN AND GLUE
~
HAZELNUTS, WALNUTS
AND PECAN NUTS
~
SMALL PINE CONES
~
UNUSUAL SEED PODS
~
CINNAMON STICKS
~
DRIED ORANGE SLICES,
SEE PAGE 10 FOR HOME-MADE VERSION
~
FLORISTS' FOAM WREATH BASE
~
CHENILLE OR SILKY CORD

A glue gun is really essential to make this decoration, as it would be slow work to use conventional adhesives. The glue gun heats a solid glue stick, which melts and is directed by the nozzle. As the glue cools, it hardens once again, taking a minute or so. Check you are using the right grade of glue; the best is the sort sold for floristry and dried flower work.

Begin by gluing the larger nuts, pine cones and seed heads in place on to the foam wreath base. With your hands, support large, heavy objects until the glue sets. Work all round the wreath base, mixing materials randomly and arranging them at different angles so the surface is not too flat. Fill the spaces between the larger objects with smaller materials, and glue some small objects to others. For the most natural effect, glue two or three of the smaller materials in little groups rather than dotting them about. Continue adding materials until you are happy with the overall appearance and the base is completely covered. Attach the length of cord in a loop at the top of the ring.

*BELOW This warm, wintry spice and nut ring looks beautiful set
against polished wood.*

LEFT *This pretty ring is very easy to make. Eucalyptus leaves dry quite quickly and retain their delicious scent for a very long time.*

Dried Apple and Eucalyptus Ring

This idea is lovely and requires no craft skills whatsoever. Ideally, make the apple rings in autumn when there are plenty of spare apples from friends' and neighbours' trees.

APPLES, PREFERABLY RED-SKINNED
~
KITCHEN KNIFE
~
SALT
~
APPLE CORER
~
WOODEN ROD OR BAMBOO CANE
~
BRANCHES OF FRESH, LARGE-LEAVED EUCALYPTUS
~
WIRE
~
THICK RED RIBBON

Slice the apples into thin rings and immediately put them into a large bowl filled with a brine solution made from 30 ml (2 tablespoons) of salt to 600 ml (1 pint) cold water. Leave to soak for about 10 minutes then remove and pat dry. Cut out the centres with a corer and thread onto a wooden rod or bamboo cane. Suspend above a gentle heat source for about a week.

Snip each eucalyptus leaf from its stalk and thread onto wire. The leaves will dry at room temperature in about a week. When the apple rings and the eucalyptus are both dry, thread them together on a long wire. Twist the wire ends to secure, and cover with a thick red ribbon to hang the decoration.

Flower Petal Balls

Several of these colourful balls look effective displayed in a large bowl, and add a pretty texture and scent. The instructions below make one large petal ball, but repeat the process for more balls or a group of smaller balls. As a gift, be sure to include a small phial of extra essential oil for refreshing the scent.

FLAT-DRIED FLOWER PETALS, SUCH AS ROSE, HYDRANGEA OR LAVENDER
~
POLYSTYRENE, PAPER, FOAM OR COTTON BALL SHAPES
~
GLUE GUN AND GLUE OR QUICK-DRYING ALL-PURPOSE ADHESIVE
~
ESSENTIAL OILS TO SUIT THE SCENT OF THE FLOWERS USED

Air-dry the flower petals as described on page 8. Rose and hydrangea petals naturally dry flat, and can be dried as loose petals or as flower heads with the petals picked off later. If you use larger petals, like those of a peony, they may have a tendency to curl, and should be dried and pressed between sheets of paper with weights on top.

Once the petals are dried, sort out a pile of petals roughly the same size, discarding any which are damaged, brown or torn. Glue the petals to a ball shape using a glue gun or adhesive, by placing glue on the ball surface and sticking each petal individually in place. The balls can be made quickly with a glue gun, but the gun may be difficult to control when attaching small petals. In this case, you may find it easier to use an adhesive. When the ball is completely covered, drop a small amount of essential oil on the ball.

To make a petal ball from tiny flower heads, such as lavender, use a conventional adhesive suitable for the material from which the ball is made (some glues react to polystyrene, for example, so should not be used for this type of ball shape). Spread the adhesive over a small area of the ball and sprinkle lavender over. Repeat until the ball is covered. Alternatively, place the lavender in a deep container and dip the glued area of the ball into the lavender, repeating until the ball is completely covered. Then add several drops of essential oil.

BELOW Colourful flower petal balls look best when made with separate types of petals on each ball, and they look beautiful displayed in bowls.

Flower-covered Rings

~

These rings are made in exactly the same way as the flower petal balls, but some larger sprigs of flowers are used and different colours are mixed together on one ring. A few whole rose buds make a good contrast in texture when scattered throughout the flatter petals on the ring. The ring can be hung from a wall by a ribbon, simply propped on a shelf, or attached to a wall or door with a small sticky fixer.

FLORISTS' FOAM RING BASE
FOR DRIED FLOWERS
~
DRIED FLOWERS OF YOUR
CHOICE, SUCH AS ROSES,
LARKSPUR AND HYDRANGEA
~
GLUE GUN AND GLUE OR QUICK-DRYING
ALL-PURPOSE ADHESIVE
~
ESSENTIAL OILS TO SUIT
THE STRONGEST SCENT OF
THE FLOWERS USED
~
RIBBON OR CORD, OPTIONAL

ABOVE Pictured here is a red rose, blue larkspur and green hydrangea flower-covered ring and a version using yellow roses and pink larkspur, but you can choose your own flower and colour combinations.

Lightweight brown foam rings are designed especially for dried flower decorations, and are available from flower shops and florists' suppliers. You can either dry the petals and flower heads yourself, see page 8, or buy them. You should have a good mix of whole flower heads and petals.

Working on a small area of the ring at a time, and working round in one direction, glue petals and clusters of flowers in random patches of colour, using the glue gun or adhesive. As with the flower petal balls, apply the glue to the ring, then stick on the petals. Do not glue petals to the back of the ring. When the foam ring is covered at the front, add a few larger buds or flower heads and a few drops of essential oil. Attach a ribbon or cord to the top of the ring, if desired. The finished ring is very lightweight and easy to hang.

Spice Pomander

The inspiration for this pomander originates from the old spice pomanders made with cloves and a pierced orange. You may prefer to use other spices and dried berries; suitable ones include green peppercorns, juniper berries, hawthorn berries, allspice and star anise.

GOOD QUANTITY LARGE CLOVES
~
GLUE GUN AND GLUE
~
5CM (2IN) DIAMETER POLYSTYRENE OR FOAM
BALL SHAPE
~
ORANGE AND CLOVE ESSENTIAL OIL, OPTIONAL
~
VELVET OR CHENILLE BRAID

Always buy more cloves than you need, as you will need to pick through them and discard any broken ones. The best cloves are large and light ginger-brown in colour.

Start by dabbing a little hot glue on the ball shape and attaching the first clove with its round head upwards. Hold it in place until the glue sets. Once you have attached a few cloves, they will support each other. Work in rows or rings neatly round the ball until it is completely covered. Add a few drops of essential oil over the surface of the cloves, and tie the ball with a length of braid or ribbon.

Cinnamon Cube

This spicy decoration is made from a cube foam base and covered with lengths of cinnamon quills. Pile several of these cubes together with each one tied with a different ribbon for an attractive effect. A single cube looks equally good, especially if it is tied with a beautiful organdie, velvet or taffeta ribbon.

LARGE SQUARE FLORISTS' FOAM FOR DRIED FLOWERS
~
KITCHEN KNIFE
~
GOOD QUANTITY CINNAMON STICKS
~
SECATEURS
~
GLUE GUN AND GLUE
~
CINNAMON ESSENTIAL OIL, OPTIONAL
~
RIBBON

Cut a cube from the foam, basing the size on the length of the cinnamon sticks you have. Cinnamon sticks cut very easily with secateurs, so you can trim them to fit the cube exactly. Cut all the cinnamon sticks to length, but remember that once you have glued some to the sides, the sticks across the top will need to be longer to cover the added thickness at the joined edges.

Using the glue gun, glue the sticks to the four sides of the cube first, butting them up close to each other, to cover the foam completely. Then glue cinnamon sticks to the top and bottom sides of the cubes, overlapping the joins at the edges. Continue until the whole cube is covered with cinnamon. Add a boost of fragrance with cinnamon essential oil, if desired, and tie with a ribbon.

You may prefer to 'cure' the scent of the cube. To do this, make a spice mixture from powdered cinnamon, cloves, nutmeg and orris root, then place the mixture in a paper bag and place the cube in the mixture. Seal the bag and leave it for a week or two in a dark place. This process adds fragrance and fixes the natural scent of cinnamon.

LEFT *A gold and blue ribbon sets off the dark tones of cloves in this spice pomander.*

RIGHT *This cinnamon cube, with its spicy fragrance, makes a perfect Christmas gift. Spice pomanders made from cloves and dried berries add to the display.*

Scented Leaf Cube
~

For this project, aromatic leaves are glued and overlapped on to a foam cube. Eucalyptus leaves are used here, but you could use any robust, scented dried leaves, such as bay or small evergreens. Smaller versions of these cubes would look pretty decorating a Christmas tree or used in an evergreen garland. The instructions below make one cube, but repeat the process for several cubes.

ABOUT 180 LEAVES DRIED EUCALYPTUS
~
9 CM (3½ IN) SQUARE CUBE OF DRY
FLORISTS' FOAM
~
GLUE GUN AND GLUE
~
1.1 METRES (3½ FEET) RED AND WHITE NARROW
PAPER RIBBON
~
70-80 DRIED GREEN PEPPERCORNS

The number of leaves you will need depends on the size of the leaves. Try to find matching leaves about 3 cm (1¼ in) long, preferably using the round-leaved eucalyptus variety.

Sort them, discarding any that are too large or too small, and set the good ones aside.

If you cannot find a cube of the proper dimensions, cut a block of foam down to size. Starting on one face of the cube, and working in rows from the bottom to the top, glue the leaves side by side with the glue gun, each leaf slightly overlapping the next and each row overlapping the one below it. On the corners you will need to wrap the leaves around if possible. Try to keep the rows neat and straight, but do not worry if they are not totally symmetrical. Continue gluing leaves until the whole cube is covered.

Cut lengths of the ribbon and wrap a strip around each face of the cube, gluing the ends where they meet and the centres where one strip crosses the other. Now glue green peppercorns along the strips of ribbon at roughly 1 cm (½ in) intervals. If you intend to hang the cube, make a loop of the red paper ribbon and glue the loop to the top centre of the cube.

BELOW Scented leaf cubes bound in red ribbon make great decorations for the Christmas season, and small versions could be tucked into evergreen wreaths or garlands.

Green Leaf Pot-pourri
~

A leaf pot-pourri makes an unusual alternative to a flower pot-pourri. The mixture of different green colours is achieved by using a range of common and exotic leaves. If you have a garden, experiment with drying all types of growing leaves. Many herbs dry well, but so do other more decorative leaves, such as scented pelargoniums. The materials listed below are given in measures, so you can choose what size measure to use according to the amount of pot-pourri you want to make.

2 MEASURES DRIED BAY LEAVES
~
2 MEASURES DRIED EUCALYPTUS LEAVES
~
2 MEASURES DRIED HERBS, SUCH AS ROSEMARY, SAGE AND LEMON VERBENA; SOME IN SPRIGS
~
1 MEASURE EXOTIC DRIED LEAVES, SUCH AS OLIVE LEAVES
~
1/2 MEASURE DRIED REINDEER MOSS
~
1/2 MEASURE POWDERED ORRIS ROOT
~
LIME, ROSEMARY AND LEMON VERBENA ESSENTIAL OILS
~
PAPER BAGS

ABOVE Eucalyptus, bay leaves, olive leaves and herbs give this pot-pourri an exotic appearance and fresh scent.

WHOLE FRESH OR DRIED LIMES, TO DECORATE
~
SHALLOW BOWL OR PLATE, OPTIONAL
~
DECORATIVE BOXES OR CELLOPHANE BAGS, OPTIONAL

In a large bowl, mix together all the leaves and moss. Add the powdered orris root and mix thoroughly. Orris root helps to fix and keep the fragrances.

Now add about 6 drops each of the essential oils, and continue to stir. Because it is difficult to be precise with the quantity of essential oils, sniff the mixture occasionally and decide when it smells right to you, adding drops of oil as necessary. Divide the pot-pourri into paper bags, loosely roll the tops closed, and store them away from light for several weeks to cure. When ready, display the pot-pourri in a shallow bowl or plate, decorate with the limes for extra texture, and display in a place where it can be seen to best advantage. If giving the pot-pourri as a present, place the mixture in small boxes or cellophane bags.

Red Rose Pot-pourri

Roses are a classic choice in pot-pourri because they always look rich and vibrant and have a wonderful scent that is immensely popular. Rather than a deep bowl to hold the pot-pourri, choose a shallow decorative plate, and wrap the whole gift in crunchy cellophane. The ingredients are given in measures, so you can choose the size of your measure according to the amount of pot-pourri you want to make.

3 MEASURES BRIGHT RED DRIED ROSE BUDS
~
1 MEASURE MINIATURE DRIED RED CHILLI PEPPERS
~
1 MEASURE SMALL DRIED POMEGRANATES
~
1/2 MEASURE POWDERED ORRIS ROOT
~
1/4 MEASURE GROUND CINNAMON
~
ROSE OR ROSE GERANIUM ESSENTIAL OIL
~
PAPER BAG
~
DECORATIVE PLATE, OPTIONAL
~
CELLOPHANE AND RED RIBBON, OPTIONAL

Place the rose buds, chilli peppers and pomegranates in a large bowl and mix in the orris root and cinnamon. Now add several drops of essential oil and continue stirring, so the oil is absorbed by the dry ingredients. Transfer the mixture to a paper bag, and loosely roll the top. Leave the bag in a dark place to cure for several weeks. Every few days, shake the bag.

When it is ready, display the pot-pourri on a shallow plate and add a little more essential oil if the fragrance still needs a boost. Then wrap the plate in thick cellophane and place it in a box before giving it as a gift. Use a large red bow to embellish the gift, if desired.

You can adapt this basic recipe by using different spices and flower ingredients; however use an oil with a fragrance in keeping with the type of flower used.

BELOW The deep-blue frosted glass plate throws the brilliant reds of rose pot-pourri into glamourous contrast.

Rose Wreath
~

This delicate and pretty wreath is made from luscious freeze-dried roses in the palest shades of apricot. Although they are expensive to buy, their quality is superb and they look like fresh roses. Combined with soft green hydrangea, the roses are glued to a foam base. If you prefer, use a different colour combination or try deep red roses with blue hydrangea or purple lavender.

1 BUNCH DRIED GREEN HYDRANGEA
~
12 FREEZE-DRIED ROSE HEADS
~
12 DRIED POPPY SEED HEADS
~
SECATEURS
~
GLUE GUN AND GLUE
~
15 CM (6 IN) DIAMETER FOAM WREATH RING FOR
DRIED FLOWERS
~
LIGHT GREEN RIBBON OR BOW

ABOVE Freeze-dried roses in a pale apricot shade make a very pretty colour scheme for this rose wreath. Here, the wreath is presented in a small green-painted wire basket lined with more hydrangea flowers.

Split the hydrangea heads into smaller florets. Cut the rose and poppy seed heads from their stems. Begin by gluing the roses in place, working round the wreath and angling them all slightly differently for the most natural and attractive effect. Once you are happy with the positioning, hold the rose heads in place until the glue has set.

Once all the roses are in place, glue a few poppy seed heads between them. Finally push the small hydrangea florets in among the other flowers, and glue them into position, filling all the remaining spaces until the front and sides of the foam wreath are totally covered with flowers. Attach a pretty bow or ribbon in a toning colour to the top to hang the wreath.

Christmas Tree Decorations

A collection of these little scented tree decorations would make a wonderful Christmas-time gift. The variations are endless once you have collected together different materials. The glue gun makes assembly quick and simple. In addition to the list of materials below, other naturally scented items, such as dried flowers, whole spices, dried herbs and seed pods, could be used.

CINNAMON STICKS
~
EUCALYPTUS AND OTHER DRIED LEAVES
~
RED ROSE HEADS
~
WHOLE CLOVES
~
WHOLE GREEN PEPPERCORNS
~
WHOLE NUTS IN THEIR SHELLS
~
SMALL PINE CONES
~
DRIED ORANGE SLICES, SEE PAGE 10 FOR HOME-MADE VERSION
~
MINIATURE DRIED POMEGRANATES

ABOVE A box of these delicate tree ornaments makes a wonderful gift, bringing the scent of the Christmas season into the home.

GLUE GUN AND GLUE OR QUICK-DRYING ALL-PURPOSE ADHESIVE
~
FINE GOLD CORD OR NARROW RED RIBBON
~
ORANGE AND CINNAMON ESSENTIAL OILS, OPTIONAL

To make one variation of these decorations, simply glue two cinnamon sticks together, then glue the ends of the cinnamon sticks to three overlapping eucalyptus leaves, attaching a dried rose bud where the leaves join the sticks. Tie on a ribbon and loop to the cinnamon sticks or alternatively glue the loop in place.

For another idea, glue a stick of cinnamon to half a slice of dried orange and glue on one or two dried rose heads. Glue on a red ribbon bow and a loop.

Experiment with further variations on the same theme, and add a few drops of an essential oil to one of the absorbent materials in the decoration, if desired.

Leaf Picture Frame

~

Dried or preserved leaves are essential for this project. They need to be soft enough not to split or break if bent around the edges of a picture frame. The leaves used here came from a collection of scented exotic leaves designed to be used as a drawer fragrance. Look for these leaves in gift and flower shops, or use unscented preserved leaves.

SELECTION OF PRESERVED SCENTED
LEAVES, PREFERABLY IN 2-3
DIFFERENT COLOURS
~
SHARP CRAFT KNIFE
~
1 SMALL WOOD, METAL OR CARD PICTURE FRAME,
WITH THE FRAME MEASURING AT LEAST
3 CM (1¹/₄ IN) WIDE ALL ROUND
~
GLUE GUN AND GLUE OR QUICK-DRYING
ALL-PURPOSE ADHESIVE
~
ESSENTIAL OILS OF YOUR CHOICE,
SEE PAGE 94, OPTIONAL

ABOVE *Large exotic scented leaves, arranged in random patterns, create an unusual and exquisite picture frame.*

If your leaves are a similar size, they can be easily overlapped to create a uniform effect. Otherwise, they can be cut into random shapes and sizes, and positioned on the frame in an attractive pattern.

Using a sharp craft knife, cut one narrow edge of a leaf across to create a straight edge. Place some glue on the frame or the leaf, whichever you prefer, and line up the straight cut edge of the leaf to the inner edge of the frame. Smooth the leaf down across the frame and wrap the excess over the edge to the back of the frame. Repeat with the other leaves, gluing them on one by one and overlapping, working round the frame in one direction. Try to use the curved edges of the leaves to overlap each other.

If necessary, neaten up the leaves on the inner edges of the frame and the back of the frame with a sharp craft knife. Essential oils can be added to the frame to boost scent, or to apply scent if your leaves are unscented.

Scented Candles in Containers

These poured candles use an easy candle-making process in which melted wax is simply poured into shells and glass containers. You may like to use other containers, such as decorative tins. A small portion of beeswax is added to the white candle wax to give the finished candles a warm cream colour. You may also like to experiment with wax dyes to create coloured candles.

CLEAN AND DRY LARGE SHELLS OR HEAVY-BASED GLASS TUMBLERS

~

COTTON WICK, DEPENDING ON THE DIAMETER OF YOUR CONTAINERS

~

WHITE CANDLE WAX GRANULES

~

PURE BEESWAX

~

DOUBLE SAUCEPAN OR A BOWL OVER A PAN OF SIMMERING WATER

~

MODELLING CLAY OR FLORAL PUTTY

~

PENCIL

~

ESSENTIAL OILS OF YOUR CHOICE, SEE PAGE 94

~

TISSUE PAPER, FOR WRAPPING

Once you know the diameter of your container, you can buy the correct size of cotton wick, simply matching your measurements to those on the packets of cotton wick. A wick of the wrong size will not burn properly, so read the information on the packet carefully.

Gently dissolve some white wax granules with a small portion of beeswax in the top of a double-saucepan; use about ten parts white wax to one part beeswax. The beeswax will add a little colour and scent to the candles. Be careful not to overheat the wax.

Cut a piece of wick about twice the length required for the container. Dip the wick into the melted wax, and leave to dry and stiffen. Now attach the waxed end of the wick to the base of the container with a small piece of modelling clay or putty, and hook the top end of the wick over a pencil lying across the container top. At this stage, scent the candle wax by adding several drops of essential oil to the molten wax.

Gently pour the melted wax into the container, and leave to cool. You may need to add a little more wax if the cooled candle shrinks too much. Any spare wax can be cooled and re-melted for other candles. For a gift, wrap the candles in tissue paper and place in a gift-wrapped box.

LEFT *A collection of miniature candles in shells look attractive when lit, but you may also like to make larger candles in glassware, which enhances the reflective quality of candlelight.*

Beeswax Candles
~

Beeswax candles burn with a lovely old-fashioned honey scent. Long used for church candles and the best slow-burning house candles, they have come back in favour with the revival of the use of candlelight to create mood and atmosphere. Beeswax candles can be made from sheets of rolled wax foundation with an impressed honeycomb pattern of tiny hexagons.

ROLLED BEESWAX SHEETS
~
LENGTHS OF COTTON WICK
~
SHARP CRAFT KNIFE
~
WIDE RIBBON AND TISSUE PAPER, OPTIONAL

To roll your own candles, tightly roll a sheet of beeswax round a length of wick, which has been cut slightly longer

ABOVE Cream- and honey-coloured beeswax candles, tied with ribbon and nestled in crisp brown tissue paper, make a simple but stunning scented gift.

than the length of your candle. You can cut the beeswax sheet to make smaller, squatter candles, or leave the sheet whole for taller candles.

If you prefer, cut a diagonal from the top left-hand corner of a beeswax sheet to about half-way down the centre of the right-hand side. Then place the wick along the long left-hand side and tightly roll up the beeswax, so the candle becomes tiered as it takes shape. Experiment with different angles of the diagonal, cut to create a variety of tiered beeswax candles.

To present the candles as a gift, tie several together into a bundle with a large ribbon bow. Wrap the bundle in tissue paper, then place the candles in a decorative but sturdy box.

FRESH FLOWER GIFTS

Fresh flowers are by far the most popular scented gift for almost any occasion. Flowers are so versatile, suitable for celebrations or commiserations, birthday presents or simple thank-you gifts. A wonderful range of scented flowers is available throughout every season of the year in flower shops, but be aware of what you are buying. A loose bunch of commercially bought cut flowers is not always a good purchase. The flowers are often badly colour matched and poorly co-ordinated; there may be quite short- stemmed blooms amidst long-stemmed flowers, which makes flower arranging difficult. If you have a garden, you will not be limited by commercial choices and can grow the flowers you like best, but you will be limited by growing seasons. An arrangement of cut flowers inserted in florists' foam in a pretty basket is a much better gift than a selection of cut flowers because the arrangement requires no further care once it reaches its destination. A tied bouquet or posy is also excellent if it has already been arranged and can just be placed in a vase. Scented bulbs or plants growing in soil make a long-lasting gift, and they can be transplanted. However you choose to present fresh flowers, do finish them off with cellophane, ribbons, bows and tissue paper to make the gift extra special and add a label instructing on the care of the flowers.

A Basket of Scented Flowers

Take a little time and trouble to create a beautiful basket of flowers. You can find a new basket or an antique one, but make sure it is nice enough to use long after the flowers have faded. The red flowers in this arrangement make a colourful impact, and are available in late spring. Choose a selection of flowers from the list below or use alternative blooms.

RED SCENTED ROSES
~
YELLOW SCENTED ROSES
~
RED ANEMONES
~
TULIPS AND RANUNCULUS IN SHADES OF RED
~
AN OBLONG BASKET WITH A HANDLE
~
SHEET OF PLASTIC OR METAL FOIL
~
FLORISTS' FOAM, CUT TO SIT
INSIDE THE BASKET
~
CELLOPHANE OR A LARGE BOW

The dramatic colour scheme is achieved by avoiding foliage as a contrast to keep the colour highly concentrated. The arrangement is designed to be viewed from the front, so the blooms are all facing forwards and ranging in height from the tallest at the back to the lowest at the front.

Cut a piece of plastic or foil slightly larger than the base of the basket and place it in the bottom of the basket, creasing into corners and with the remaining edges of plastic or foil reaching a little way up the sides. Soak the florists' foam well, and place it in the bottom of the basket.

Insert the tallest blooms at the back to set the outline and height of the arrangement. Continue adding blooms close together, leaving no space between the flowers, to create a rich, textured look. Continue adding flowers until the basket is filled. Wrap the entire arrangement in cellophane, or tie a ribbon bow on the handle of the basket.

RIGHT *This predominantly red flower arrangement displays red roses, anemones, tulips and ranunculus, accented by yellow roses.*

Primrose Collection
~

This arrangement uses a trug as the container. A trug is an old-fashioned wooden basket designed to carry plants, tools or seeds. Most countries have their own particular design and shape, and the small-scale versions are perfect for growing plants. Spring flowers are always enchanting and primroses are some of the prettiest, combining simple but beautiful flowers with a fresh and lovely scent.

SMALL WOODEN TRUG OR BASKET
~
PALE YELLOW, ONE-COAT MATT PAINT
~
PRIMROSE PLANTS
~
HAND DRILL
~
MOSS
~
POTTING COMPOST, OPTIONAL
~
WIRE-EDGED YELLOW
GINGHAM RIBBON

ABOVE A collection of growing primroses are planted inside a French-style gardening trug, and have a fresh outdoor appearance.

If you want the plants to be displayed in the container for some time, make proper drainage holes and plant the primroses in potting compost. If the basket is to hold the primroses temporarily, then the plants can stay in their plastic pots and simply be covered with moss on the top surface.

To make drainage holes, drill three or four small holes in the base of the trug. Paint the whole trug with the matt yellow paint and leave to dry. A one-coat variety of paint requires no separate undercoat.

Now put a little potting compost in the trug, knock the primroses from their pots, and plant the flowers inside the trug. Alternatively, group the plants in their pots inside the trug, angling them if necessary to make them look as natural as possible. With either method, finish with a layer of loose or bun moss on the surface, and tie a big yellow gingham bow on the handle.

Hyacinth Bulbs in a Painted Pot

Hyacinths in bloom are marvellous decorative additions to the house in winter and spring. The flowers last for a long time and bring fragrance and colour at a time when both are scarce in the garden. If you are organised, you can plant your own hyacinth bulbs to flower when you choose, after giving them the necessary period of cold and dark conditions. This way you can have the pick of the many colours and varieties available through catalogues and nurseries. However, you can use hyacinths already in bud and growing singly in pots, available in the basic colour ranges of blue, white or pink.

SMALL TERRACOTTA POTS
OR ONE LARGE POT
~
PAINT PIGMENT AND
PAINT MEDIUM, OR
ONE-COAT MATT PAINT
~
PAINTBRUSHES
~
GROWING HYACINTHS
~
LOOSE MOSS
~
EXTRA POTTING COMPOST OR
BULB FIBRE, IF REQUIRED
~
BOW AND LABEL, OPTIONAL

ABOVE Some of these terracotta pots have been painted with green pigment colours to give a natural effect that highlights the colour of the hyacinths.

To colour a plain terracotta pot, mix the paint pigment with an oil- or water-based medium to create a colour specially tailored to your requirements. Oil-based mediums soak into the pot, carrying a little colour with them, and give an interesting natural finish.

Alternatively, use a matt paint of any kind, but this will give a more solid and opaque finish. Paint the pot and leave until completely dry.

Either plant a single hyacinth into a small pot or group several together into a larger container. Generally, an odd number of bulbs looks most effective, but it will depend on the shape and size of container you use. Add extra potting compost if required. Put a layer of moss over the top to cover the compost, and add a bow and a label describing the care needed for the hyacinths.

ABOVE This mauve-coloured posy is best displayed in a simple, plain container such as a wine glass or goblet.

A Mauve- and Cream-coloured Posy

Giving a posy of flowers is not a new idea, and a tied bunch of scented blooms is a delightful gift to receive. This scented posy has a subtle colour scheme of mauve and cream, and is tied with a big rosette ribbon bow. The posy is tied high under the flower heads, leaving the stems fairly long so the finished bunch can be tucked into a drinking glass.

1 CREAM TULIP OR ROSE

5 MAUVE FREESIAS

5 CREAM FREESIAS

5 MAUVE TULIPS

1 BUNCH CREAM DOUBLE NARCISSI

THIN WIRE OR STRING

10 ARUM LEAVES OR ANY SPEAR-SHAPED LEAF

WIRE-EDGED MAUVE RIBBON

Use a cream rose or tulip as the central flower, and hold it in one hand. Then add a circle of alternating mauve and cream freesias around the central flower. For the next circle of flowers, introduce some mauve tulips and cream narcissi.

Continue adding flowers until they are all used. Tie the stems with wire or string, then take the green arum leaves and place them round the posy to make a frill of green. Tie the posy once again with wire or string to secure. Trim a small amount off the stems to make most of them equal, but do not worry if a few are shorter than the rest. Place the posy in a vase with a little water and set aside.

To make the rosette bow, make a loop of ribbon and hold it tight while you make another. Continue making more loops of the same size and catching hold of them until you have a full rosette. Now wrap the bases of the loops with a piece of wire, and pull it tight to catch them all together. Open out the rosette to make a pretty shape, and cut each end of the ribbon into a V. Attach the ribbon with wire to the wire around the posy stems.

A Medieval-inspired Posy
~

This pretty posy is special enough to be carried by a brides-
maid or even a bride. It has a neat and formal look, but the
trails of threaded stephanotis give it a glamorous touch. The
scent is alluring, with powerfully fragrant freesias alongside
the stephanotis. It is usually most economical to cut stephan-
otis flowers from a growing plant; this bouquet used two
flowering plants to provide enough open flowers for the
strings of blooms.

2 STEPHANOTIS PLANTS
TO GIVE ABOUT
35 BLOOMS
~
REEL WIRE
~
1 BUNCH CHINCHERINCHEES
~
10 WHITE RANUNCULUS
~
12 STEMS CREAM FREESIAS
~
GOLD GAUZE RIBBON
~
GOLD CORD

ABOVE *The handle of this stephanotis posy is wrapped with gold*
ribbon and cord to give it a medieval look.

Cut off all the stephanotis flowers and thread them on to
wire, one behind the other, twisting a knot at the end to
stop the first bloom falling off. Make three of these flower
strings and leave a length of bare wire at the end to become
part of the posy handle.

Now make the posy by holding the bunch of chincherinchees for the centre, and adding a circle of ranunculus,
followed by a circle of freesias. If the flowers are difficult to
hold in your hand, tie the stems together with wire after
completing each new circle of flowers. Arrange the strands
of stephanotis at one side of the posy and bring their wire
stems into the main posy stem.

Make a rosette of gauze ribbon (see page 32) and arrange
this at the bottom of the stems. Wrap another length
of ribbon round the stems, from the bottom to the top,
covering the rosette ribbon ends. Now wrap a length
of gold cord, criss-crossing the handle, knotting it at the
top and bottom.

Fresh Flower Wreath

A mixture of flowers and foliage makes up this pretty pink and cream wreath, highlighted with lime green. The method for making this wreath is very simple and can be used for any flowers you have available. You can alter the colour scheme if you prefer, but remember to vary the size and shapes of the materials to give an interesting finished texture. For example, a head or two of a large-flowered lily will make all the difference to the look of the final wreath.

FLORISTS' FOAM WREATH BASE
~
2 PALE PINK LILIES
~
12 PALE PINK ROSES
~
8 PINK RANUNCULUS
~
12 PINK SPRAY CARNATIONS
~
1 STEM VIBURNUM OPULUS
~
2 STEMS WHITE CHERRY BLOSSOM
~
3 STEMS GREEN HELLEBORE
~
3 STEMS GREEN FOLIAGE, SUCH AS PHILADELPHUS
~
WIDE PINK RIBBON
~
WIRE

Soak the wreath base until it is completely wet. This is very important, as there is only a small area of foam to keep all the flowers in the wreath damp. Cut the flowers and shrubs into short pieces using secateurs or shears, but leave enough stem to push right into the foam, with the flowers flat against the surface.

To make the hellebores last well after the stems are cut, stand them in a small amount of boiling water for about 3 minutes. This seals the ends and keeps the flowers fresh.

Make the basis of the wreath green by inserting a layer of foliage into the foam wreath, covering it with the philadelphius and hellebore. Ideally hang the wreath on a wall or door so you can get an idea of how the wreath will look hanging up. If this is difficult to do, lay the wreath flat while you work on it, but decide at the outset which is to be the top and bottom.

Next insert the less important flowers in the wreath, starting with the spray carnations and ranunculus. These can be spaced evenly round the wreath. Remember to vary the angle of the flowers and arrange some inside the ring edge and some round the outside edge. Then insert the roses in place, choosing carefully where they should go for maximum effect.

Insert the lilies into the wreath, in this case diagonally oppposite each other on the circle. Finally fill in any gaps with small pieces of flowering cherry blossom and viburnum opulus, and use more foliage if areas of foam are still showing through.

Check that the lower inside edge of the wreath is well-covered as this will show when the wreath is displayed. Add a wire loop at the top of the wreath for hanging it.

To give the wreath as a present, wrap it loosely in cellophane or plastic to keep it moist, and suggest that the person who is receiving the present sprays the flowers regularly with water to keep the wreath fresh and fragrant for as long as possible.

LEFT AND RIGHT Large-flowered lilies provide the focal points for this beautiful scented wreath, but you can choose flowers according to their availability during the season.

Cream and White Bouquet

White lilac sprays are combined with pale green viburnum opulus and crisp white and yellow irises in a large loose bouquet. Trails of small-leaved variegated ivy fall gracefully and soften the whole effect. The bouquet looks attractive placed in a glass or porcelain vase, and is glamorous enough to be carried as a bride's bouquet.

4 STEMS WHITE LILAC
~
4 STEMS GREEN VIBURNUM OPULUS
~
10 WHITE IRISES
~
4 WHITE TULIPS
~
TRAILS OF CREAM VARIEGATED
SMALL-LEAVED IVY
~
SOFT STRING TO TIE STEMS
~
CREAM OR WHITE ORGANZA RIBBON

ABOVE *The white and cream colours create a romantic theme for this flower and ivy bouquet.*

This large bouquet is made in the hand just like the smaller flower posies on pages 32-33. Begin by trimming all the stems to the same length. Although you can choose any flower for the centre of the arrangement because they will all be mixed together, do arrange each type of flower fairly evenly throughout the bouquet.

Add flowers in rings around the centre flowers, working your way round in a circle. As you add each stem, twist it slightly so the stems start to spiral. This will keep the heads of the flowers loose and open and the bunch as full as possible. Add some ivy strands to the edge of the bouquet, then tie the finished bunch with string, about one-third of the way down the stems. Finally, add a large bow with flowing ends of ribbon, tying it over the string.

Scented Spring Posy

A mixture of spring garden flowers are included in this colour-ful posy. Along with tiny sweet violets and primroses in several colours, there are a few sprigs of sweet-smelling osmanthus delavayii with small evergreen leaves and a few stems of a heavily scented purple wallflower. Alternatively you may like to choose dianthus, sweet peas, mignonette, scented geraniums and roses.

PRIMROSES
~
VIOLETS
~
WALLFLOWERS
~
OSMANTHUS DELAVAYII
~
STRING
~
RIBBON BOW

Hold a bunch of one of the flowers in your hand and add individual flowers or small groups of flowers, working your way in a circle round the outside of the centre bunch. Continue until you have a well-balanced but small posy. Tie the stems with soft string and trim the stem ends to make them neat and even.

Decorate with a ribbon bow. Try to keep the posy in water until the last possible moment to preserve its fresh-ness. You can wrap the ends of the stems in plastic film or metal foil, but this may spoil the posy's appearance and detract from its simple, newly-picked look.

BELOW A spring posy made from tiny flowers makes a charming miniature arrangement which can be tucked informally into a small container.

Gifts For The Bedroom

Everyone loves to receive luxurious and beautiful presents for their own personal use, and even a person with normally austere taste will usually appreciate something a little lacy or glamorous to tuck into a drawer or hang in a wardrobe. Making your own scented gifts for the bedroom means that you can use very beautiful fabrics and materials, choose colours which you know will be appreciated, and tailor fragrances to suit the eventual owner.

Most of the ideas in this chapter use small amounts of fabric. Although some will demand a little skill with a needle and thread, they are not very difficult to put together. Buy small remnants of silk or pretty print fabrics when you see them in shops, and keep scraps from other sewing projects. Synthetic waddings and stuffings are the cleanest and easiest materials to use for padding gifts such as hangers, and small pieces of fragrance-soaked cotton wool or scoops of natural pot-pourri can be placed in the wadding to add scent. Take care and trouble to wrap the finished gifts beautifully and in a sympathetic way for the present inside. If you have scented the gift with essential oils or perfume oils, then include a small bottle of the oil with the gift, so the fragrance can be replenished from time to time.

Linen Cupboard Lavender Bags

These sachets are large enough to slide between sheets and towels while airing. Lavender is a traditional wash-day herb and brings a clean fresh scent to laundry and linen. The sachet can also double as a sleep pillow, or form part of a group of pretty pillows on a bed. Crisp white cotton and lace have been combined with a small navy and white checked fabric for a smart but feminine look.

READY-MADE, WHITE CUT-AWAY LACE TABLE MATS
IN PAIRS
~
NAVY AND WHITE CHECKED COTTON FABRIC
~
SEWING SCISSORS
~
SEWING MACHINE
~
WHITE SEWING THREAD
~
SYNTHETIC WADDING
~
LAVENDER POT-POURRI, SEE PAGE 39,
OR DRIED LAVENDER
~
LAVENDER ESSENTIAL OIL
~
THIN LENGTHS OF NAVY RIBBON, OPTIONAL

White lace table mats, either round or oblong, are used as an outer covering to the lavender-filled navy checked sachet inside. Measure the white table mats and cut two circles or oblongs a bit smaller than the table mats from the navy checked fabric. With right sides facing, sew the fabric pieces round three sides, then turn right-way out, and press the seams. Fill the sachet with wadding to give a soft, but not full, effect. Then mix a few drops of essential oil with the dried lavender, and spoon into the sachet. Sew up the fourth side by hand.

Place the white lace mats together with the decorative sides facing each other. Sew along three sides. Turn right-way out, press the seams, and slide in the scented sachet. Finally, sew the fourth side closed by hand, using a tiny hidden stitch.

To make little fabric sachets, cut small oblongs or squares from the checked fabric. With right sides facing, sew round three sides, as above, and fill with dried lavender and wadding in the same way. Either sew up the final side by hand, or tie the sachets with ribbon to make a bag shape. These crisp square sachets make ideal gifts for men and can be stowed away in a sock drawer or a suitcase to keep clothes fresh.

Lavender Pot-pourri
~

Use this mixture for the Linen Cupboard Bags or display the pot-pourri in a decorative bowl.

2 CUPS LAVENDER FLOWERS
~
1/2 CUP MIXED LARKSPUR AND CORNFLOWER PETALS
~
10 ML (2 TEASPOONS) POWDERED ORRIS ROOT
~
4 DROPS LAVENDER ESSENTIAL OIL
~
PAPER BAG

ABOVE These fragrant linen bags, pillows and sachets can be used to scent linen, drawers and wardrobes. The large decorative sachets look beautiful displayed on a bed with other white lacy pillows.

Mix the flowers and orris root in a bowl and add the drops of essential oil, stirring to combine. Transfer the mixture to a paper bag, loosely seal, and place in a cool dry place to cure for four to six weeks, shaking the bag occasionally.

Jewellery Bags and Rolls

These small bags are designed to hold jewellery, tights or cosmetics, and are especially useful to pack into luggage when travelling. For further reference, see the diagrams on pages 92-93.

REMNANTS OF BRIGHTLY
COLOURED SILK
OR SATIN
~
SEWING SCISSORS
~
SEWING MACHINE
~
SEWING THREADS TO
MATCH YOUR FABRIC
~
THIN SYNTHETIC WADDING
~
ESSENTIAL OILS
OF YOUR CHOICE,
SEE PAGE 94
~
RIBBONS OR CORDS

ABOVE *Silk jewellery bags in various shapes make beautiful and useful presents. These variations are, from left to right, the Folded Wallet, the Envelope and the Roll.*

The Roll

Cut two pieces of silk, 38 x 13 cm (15 x 5 in). With right sides facing, sew round two long sides and one short side. Turn right sides out, and press the seams. Fill with a thin layer of wadding scented with a few drops of essential oil. Sew the fourth side neatly closed by hand (diag. A).

Cut three 8.75 cm square (3½ in square) pieces from the same fabric. Hem all four edges of each square with a narrow hem. Pin the squares, right sides up, to one side of the padded oblong to make pockets. Pin them at equal distances from each other and all edges of the oblong. Leave an open end on each square; all open ends of the pockets should face the same short end of the oblong. Sew the pockets on to the oblong by hand through one layer of fabric (diag. B).

Sew a length of cord or ribbon to the middle of the narrow end (diag. C). The bag is then rolled up towards the short, corded end and the cord wraps round the roll and ties the bag closed at the top (diag. D).

The Envelope

Cut two pieces of silk, 38 x 15 cm (15 x 6 in). Cut an apex in both pieces at one of the short ends, from 13 cm (5 in) along each long side up to the middle of the short side (diag. A).

Place right sides together and sew up all round the oblong, except for the remaining straight short side. Turn right sides out and press seams. Fill with scented wadding and sew the short side closed by hand. Fold up the bottom straight short side to meet the point where the apex end begins. Sew in place along the sides to form a pocket (diag. B). Use special binding ribbon, or press a ribbon in half lengthways. Pin the ribbon all round the edges from the bottom corner, round the apex point to the bottom of the other side of the envelope. Turn under both raw edges of the ribbon at the bottom. Sew the binding ribbon in place all round the envelope (diag. C).

Fold the apex point down over the pocket to close the envelope and mark the point where the apex meets the envelope pocket. Sew on a length of ribbon to the point of the apex and another length of ribbon to the outside of the pocket, so the envelope can be tied closed (diag. D).

Folded Wallet

~

Cut two pieces of silk, 28 cm square (11 in square). Make another oblong shape, as before, padded with scented wadding. Fold one short edge up 10 cm (4 in) and sew the sides closed to form a large pocket (diag. A). Divide this large pocket into three smaller ones by sewing two vertical seams, from the top edge to the bottom, through all thicknesses of silk and wadding (diag. B).

Fold the remaining flap over the pocket opening. Sew a length of wide ribbon round the back of the wallet, leaving two loose ends (diag. C). The wallet is then folded in half like a book, and the ribbon tied into a bow to hold the wallet closed (diag. D).

Satin Drawstring Bag

~

This pretty bag could be used to store tights, cosmetics or hair dressing equipment. The little padded heart contains wadding scented with essential oil. Always take care when scenting the wadding. Wrap the scented piece in another clean piece, and make sure the oil has been absorbed before you stuff the fabric, to avoid staining the satin. If you prefer, use a small amount of wadding and a scoop of well-scented pot-pourri. For further reference, see the diagrams on pages 92-93.

ABOUT 1 METRE (1 YARD) SATIN FABRIC
~
SEWING SCISSORS
~
SEWING MACHINE
~
SEWING THREADS IN A COLOUR TO MATCH YOUR FABRIC
~
SYNTHETIC WADDING
~
ESSENTIAL OILS OF YOUR CHOICE, SEE PAGE 94, OR ANY SUITABLE POT-POURRI
~
FLAT RIBBON
~
CORD OR ROUND SECTION RIBBON
~
MATCHING OR CONTRASTING TASSEL

Cut two pieces of satin fabric, each measuring 20 x 47 cm (8 x 19 in). With right sides facing, sew down the two long sides to make a tube, leaving a 3.5 cm (1½ in) gap in each seam, 19 cm (7½ in) from the top (diag. A).

ABOVE A scented satin bag makes a luxurious gift and is a perfect container for a shop-bought present, such as a piece of jewellery or a little trinket.

Cut a circle of satin for the base, 15 cm (6 in) in diameter, and, with the right side facing inside the tube, sew it round the bottom of the tube with the seams on the outside. Gather up the fabric if necessary (diag. B). Turn the bag right-way out. At 12 cm (5 in) from the open end of the tube, fold the top down inside the tube and press the fold.

Now make a channel for the drawstring by sewing two seams horizontally round the bag, one above and one below the gaps in the side seams, sewing the inner and outer layers of satin together (diag. C). Thread through enough flat ribbon to go round the channel twice, plus extra for the loops to be pulled through the gaps on either side, like handles. Tie the loose ends of ribbon together (diag. D).

Now cut two heart-shaped pieces of satin, about 10 cm (4 in) in height. With right sides together, sew round the edges, leaving a small gap for stuffing. Turn the heart right-way out, and fill with scented wadding or pot-pourri. Attach the tassel and heart to the bag with lengths of round section ribbon or cord.

Scented Wood Shapes
~

All types of wood readily soak up oils, unless they have been painted with impermeable paint or varnish. There are many ready-scented wooden shapes, such as carved fruits, on the market, but very few use really good perfumes. By making your own collections of shapes you are in control of how the objects look and smell.

WOODEN SHAPES OF ALL KINDS
~
ESSENTIAL OILS OF YOUR CHOICE, SEE PAGE 94
~
TISSUE PAPER
~
WOODEN CONTAINERS OR BASKETS, OPTIONAL

Turned wooden balls, fruit and vegetable shapes, flat cut-outs, carved ethnic shapes, carved animal shapes or wooden eggs are suitable for scenting. Apply drops of oil to the shapes, repeating the process a few times. Wrap in tissue paper and leave in a dark place for a few days.

If you can only find painted wooden shapes, then drill a narrow hole from a point in the object, such as the top of an apple shape, and drop the oil into the centre. Leave to soak in, and repeat a few times for the scent to impregnate.

Arrange a mixture of different shapes and sizes, or stick to one theme, such as fruit shapes or round ball shapes in varying sizes. Find a shallow box, turned wooden bowl or even just a basket to hold the collection.

Cedarwood Raspings and Sachets
~

Cedarwood has a wonderful earthy, forest smell. Its fresh clean tang is considered masculine, but the scent is also warm and comforting. It has long been used to deter insects from cupboards, and it keeps stored objects from smelling musty and old. At one time, chests and cupboards were made from or lined with the wood itself. Fill small sachets with raspings or display raspings in boxes for a simple gift idea.

CEDARWOOD RASPINGS
~
SMALL WOODEN BOXES WITH LIDS
~
HAND DRILL
~
MUSLIN SQUARES
~
WHITE SEWING THREAD
~
SEWING SCISSORS
~
SEWING MACHINE
~
PINKING SHEARS, OPTIONAL
~
NARROW RIBBONS

Little boxes filled with cedarwood raspings make delightful gifts and can be placed in cupboards or drawers, or displayed on a dresser or chest of drawers. Simply drill several tiny holes in the lid of a small wooden box to allow the scent to escape, and fill the box with raspings. You may also be able to find wooden boxes which already have perforations on the lid for this purpose.

To make sachets, fold a square of muslin and sew up one short side and the long side. Turn inside out, and trim the open edge with a pinking shears for a decorative cut, or leave the edges raw. Fill with raspings and tie with a thin ribbon. Alternatively, place the raspings directly in the centre of a muslin square and pull the edges together, tying with ribbon to close.

LEFT *Scented wooden shapes displayed in a wooden bowl or box make a rustic-looking decoration or centrepiece.*

Cedar-scented Shoe Trees
~

Although you can purchase cedarwood shoe trees, you may like to scent shoe trees that are made from other woods. These shoe trees make an excellent gift for men. You may also like to try other essential oils for scenting, such as patchouli, sandalwood or cypress.

WOODEN SHOE TREES
~
CEDARWOOD ESSENTIAL OIL
~
TISSUE PAPER OR A SUITABLE BOX
~
RIBBON

ABOVE *Wooden shoe trees scented with cedarwood or sandalwood, and decorative boxes filled with cedarwood raspings have an aroma men will appreciate.*

Apply several drops of cedarwood essential oil to the shoe trees and let the oil soak in. Repeat three or four times more, until the wood smells strongly of the oil. Wrap the shoe trees in tissue paper or place them in a lidded box. Leave the shoe trees in a dark place for a few days to dry off completely. When dry, tie the shoe trees together with a pretty length of ribbon, and wrap them in the tissue paper, if desired.

Sweet Powder Mixture

Centuries ago, sweet-smelling mixtures of herbs, flowers and spices were ground into a coarse powder and used to scent cupboards and linen. If you have a small electric coffee or spice mill, it is easy to create this basic sweet powder mixture.

1 CUP DRIED RED ROSE PETALS
~
1 CUP DRIED LAVENDER
~
5 CINNAMON STICKS
~
30 ML (2 TABLESPOONS) POWDERED ORRIS ROOT
~
15 ML (1 TABLESPOON) ALLSPICE
~
15 ML (1 TABLESPOON) BROWN SUGAR
~
15 ML (1 TABLESPOON) DRIED ORANGE PEEL
~
15 ML (1 TABLESPOON) DRIED LEMON PEEL
~
5 ML (1 TEASPOON) CLOVES
~
5 ML (1 TEASPOON) MACE
~
5 TONKA BEANS
~
1 VANILLA POD
~
FEW DROPS BRANDY

Grind all the ingredients except the brandy in small batches in an electric spice or coffee mill, tipping each batch into a large bowl. Once all the ingredients have been ground, stir the whole mixture very well to distribute evenly. Add a few drops of brandy, and stir in, but do not let the mixture get too damp. Use the mixture to fill sachets and bags.

Sweet Powder Sachets

An assortment of satin, lace and beaded sachets hold a plain inner cambric sachet filled with spice powders. The cambric sachet protects the decorative outer covering from the spice powder mixture. These sachets can be made in any size or shape you choose. Scraps of antique lace and beadwork can be incorporated into the sachet for a really romantic look.

CLOSELY WOVEN CAMBRIC FABRIC
~
SEWING SCISSORS
~
SEWING MACHINE
~
SEWING THREAD
~
SWEET POWDER MIXTURE, SEE LEFT
~
DECORATIVE PIECES OF FABRIC, SUCH AS SILK,
SATIN, LACE, BEADED PIECES AND EXTRA-WIDE
SATIN RIBBON
~
ASSORTMENT OF RIBBONS

Make cambric sachets to hold the sweet powder mixture. Cut two pieces of the cambric in the shape you want the final sachet to be. Sew the two pieces together, leaving a small gap, and turn out. Fill the cambric with the sweet powder and sew up the gap by hand. Alternatively, simply fold a square of cambric in half, sew up two sides, then turn out and fill with sweet powder mixture, sewing up the open end by hand.

To make the outer decorative covering, cut the same shape a little bigger all round from two pieces of satin, silk or lace. Beaded or lace pieces can be sewn directly on to the right side of a satin or silk piece and used as a decorative front to a sachet.

With right sides together, sew up all round three edges. Turn right-way out, press the seams lightly, and slip in the cambric sachet. Fold the open edges down inside the sachet and tie closed with a ribbon. If you are using wide ribbon, simply fold a length in half with right sides together, sew up the long sides, turn right sides out and fill with a smaller scented cambric sachet.

LEFT Use small pieces of antique lace or beadwork to bring an old-fashioned look to sweet powder sachets.

Sleep Pillows

Sleep pillows can be filled with many different ingredients according to the effect you wish to achieve. You may like a soothing, pleasant fragrance of flowers or the more heady aroma of dried hops. Certain herbs are often recommended to help an insomniac, while others help relaxation after a stress-ful day. In addition to the herbs and oils listed below, you could try single scents or mixtures of rosemary, sweet woodruff, lemon thyme, lemon verbena, lavender or mint. Dried orange peel can also be included.

COTTON FABRICS IN CO-ORDINATING DESIGNS
AND COLOURS
~
SEWING SCISSORS
~
SEWING MACHINE
~
SEWING THREADS IN COLOURS TO MATCH
YOUR FABRIC
~
DRIED HOPS
~
DRIED HERBS AND ESSENTIAL OILS, SUCH AS
CHAMOMILE, CLARY SAGE OR MARJORAM
~
SYNTHETIC WADDING
~
RIBBONS

Cut two squares of fabric to the dimensions you desire and, with right sides together, sew up three sides. Turn right sides out and press the seams. Mix up a large scoop of dried herbs and hops, adding a few drops of essential oil.

Stuff the square loosely with wadding, adding the scoop of dried ingredients to the centre of the pillow. Sew up the final side by hand with a tiny hidden stitch. You may like to reduce the quantity of wadding or eliminate it altogether, filling the pillow completely with herbs and hops.

You could also make a scented sleep pillow to slip inside a shop-bought pillow case. Simply measure your pillow case and make the herb-filled pillow, as above, to slightly smaller dimensions so it comfortably fits the case. This variation is convenient for laundering the pillow case and enables you to remove the inner herb pillow to refresh the scent.

You may also like to attach scented sachets to larger ordinary pillows and cushions, using ribbon. Make up some sachets as described in the method for the Sweet Powder Sachets (see page 44), and fill them with a mixture of dried hops and herbs mixed with a few drops of essential oil, if desired. Tie ribbon round the sachet as if you were tying up a parcel and tie a bow at the top of the sachet. Sew the bow to a large pillow. Alternatively, tie ribbon round a large pillow and tuck a sachet under one band of the ribbon.

LEFT *Scented sleep pillows can be made in any fabric you choose to suit your bedroom. Filled with dried herbs and hops, they are a great gift for an insomniac.*

Long Scented Drawer Rolls

These long stuffed roll shapes are useful to line an edge in a drawer, and give more scent than a smaller sachet. You can make them any size you choose, and simply sew the ends closed or tie one end or both ends with a ribbon. Use rich fabrics, such as these silk dupions in glowing and unusual shades of turquoise green.

SCRAPS OF SILK DUPION
~
SEWING SCISSORS
~
SEWING MACHINE
~
SEWING THREADS TO MATCH THE COLOUR OF
YOUR FABRIC
~
LOOSE WADDING
~
ESSENTIAL OILS OR LOOSE POT-POURRI
~
RIBBONS

Cut one long strip of fabric at least 45 cm (18 in) long and about 20 cm (8 in) wide. Fold the fabric with right sides together and stitch along the long raw edge to make a long tube. If you want only one tied end, sew up one of the short raw edges too.

Turn right sides out and press the seams. Turn the short raw edges, or the one short edge if you have sewn up the other, down inside the tube. Scent the wadding with a few drops of essential oil or by mixing it with pot-pourri and stuff the tube with the scented wadding.

Tie short lengths of ribbon at each end of the tube, or at the single raw end, making sure that the raw edges inside are below the point where the ribbon is tied. You may also like to add a delicate artificial fabric flower and attach it to the ribbon.

BELOW A trio of these long drawer rolls would make a lovely gift. Use brightly coloured silks with ribbons in a contrasting colour.

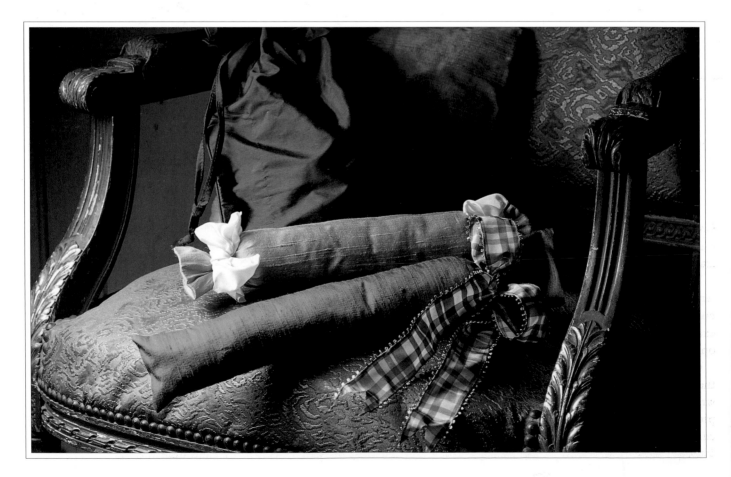

Padded Hot-water Bottle Cover

A hot-water bottle cover may seem an old-fashioned gift, but many people with the warmest bedrooms still enjoy this personal luxury to soothe aching limbs or keep feet warm. A cover is essential for comfort, so there is an opportunity to add fragrance with a little scented sachet slipped into a pocket on the outside of the cover. The scent from the sachet is released by the heat of the water in the bottle. You can find many ready-quilted fabrics available, but padding your own fabric gives you greater choice of design and colour. Use a fairly hard-wearing but smooth-surfaced fabric, such as a strong cotton or linen.

HOT WATER BOTTLE
~
PAPER AND PENCIL
~
STRONG COTTON OR LINEN FABRIC FOR THE COVER AND SACHET
~
CONTRASTING FABRIC FOR THE POCKET
~
THIN- TO MEDIUM-WEIGHT SYNTHETIC WADDING IN A SHEET
~
SEWING SCISSORS
~
SEWING MACHINE
~
MATCHING SEWING THREAD
~
LOOSE WADDING FOR SACHETS
~
LENGTHS OF RIBBON
~
ESSENTIAL OILS OF YOUR CHOICE, SEE PAGE 94, OR POT-POURRI

ABOVE The aroma from the scented sachet is released when the hot-water bottle is filled with hot water and the padded cover makes a unique home-made gift.

Choose a fabric with a pattern which has shapes you can cut out and stuff for the scenting sachet, such as a flower and fruit print fabric.

Trace roughly round the hot-water bottle to make a paper template, leaving extra room round the sides for seams and a comfortable fit. Do not follow the shape of the bottle exactly, but bring the sides up to a shallow point at the top opening where the ribbon will be attached.

Cut four pieces of fabric and two pieces of wadding, using the template as a guide. Pin one sheet of wadding to one wrong-side piece of fabric. Then, place the right side of this piece to the right side of another fabric piece. Stitch carefully round the edges through the thicknesses of wadding and fabric, leaving a gap through which you can turn the piece right-way out. Remove the pins, and turn the fabric right sides out. Carefully sew up the gap and repeat with the other two pieces of fabric and the sheet of wadding. Now you will have two padded sides.

Sew these two side pieces together along the bottom and sides, stopping where the the point begins. Turn inside out. Cut a piece of contrasting fabric for the pocket and sew this in place on one side, tucking the raw edges under slightly as you stitch. Attach a length of ribbon to both sides of the apex point at the top of the cover to tie the cover closed.

Now make the little scented sachets. Cut shapes from scraps of the main fabric and, with right sides facing, sew two pieces together round the shape, leaving a small gap in the seam. Turn the shape right sides out and stuff with loose, scented wadding, pot-pourri or sweet powder. Sew up the gap by hand using a tiny hidden stitch.

Padded Hanger and Sachet

Here, the covering fabric is gathered on to the hanger, giving a soft, ruched effect. You can use any fabric for the covering, such as cotton, silk, linen or satin, for example. Here, a pretty fresh glazed chintz makes a co-ordinating collection, each with their individual scenting bags. Fill sachets with wadding or use a dried herb mixture based on herbs suitable for the wardrobe, such as southernwood, tansy, rosemary and lavender.

STANDARD WOODEN HANGER
~
FABRIC FOR COVER AND SACHET
~
QUICK-DRYING, ALL-PURPOSE ADHESIVE
~
SYNTHETIC WADDING IN A SHEET
~
SEWING SCISSORS
~
SEWING MACHINE
~
SEWING THREAD IN
COLOURS TO MATCH
YOUR FABRIC
~
ESSENTIAL OILS OF YOUR CHOICE,
SEE PAGE 94, OR POT-POURRI
~
COTTON WOOL
~
NARROW RIBBON

ABOVE The scent of these ruched calico hangers can be replenished by simply adding new pot-pourri or scented wadding to the sachets.

Cut out a piece of the fabric to completely cover the hanger and a long bias-cut strip to cover the handle. Dab a little adhesive all over the hook. Fold the bias strip in half and, starting from the top of the hook, wrap the strip round the hook, overlapping the raw edges. Twist the end of the strip round the hook at the bottom, and secure in place with a few stitches.

Wrap a piece of wadding round the hanger, cutting a hole for the hook to pass through. Sew the wadding at the sides and bottom to hold it secure. Fold the fabric for the hanger in half lengthwise, and place the hanger on it. Bring the edges together at the top and pin in place, making a small hem with the raw edges. Now sew by hand with small gathering stitches right round the hanger, drawing up the surplus fabric as you go. Work from the hook right round to the beginning with one piece of thread.

To make the sachet, cut a square of fabric and fold with right sides together. Sew up one long side and one short side, turn right sides out and press the seams. Fold the open end down inside the sachet, and stuff the sachet with pot-pourri or wadding that has been scented with drops of essential oil. Attach the sachet to the hook of the hanger with narrow ribbon.

Embroidered Calico Hanger

~

Padded hangers are best for most clothes, but they are expensive to buy ready-made. They do make the most marvellous gift though, as no one seems to have too many. A pretty embroidered hanger stuffed with scented wadding is perfect for storing a special lacy shirt or favourite summer dress. If the embroidery seems difficult to execute, buy a fabric with a raised pattern or sew on ready-made embroidered panels or appliqué.

1 STANDARD WOODEN HANGER
~
PAPER AND PENCIL
~
CREAM-COLOURED CALICO
~
SEWING SCISSORS
~
SEWING MACHINE
~
SEWING THREAD
~
CREAM-COLOURED COTTON
EMBROIDERY THREAD
~
NARROW CREAM BRAID
~
EMBROIDERY HOOP OR FRAME
~
WADDING IN A SINGLE SHEET
~
ESSENTIAL OILS OF YOUR CHOICE, SEE PAGE 94
~
COTTON WOOL
~
CREAM-COLOURED COTTON TAPE
~
CREAM AND BLUE RIBBON

Make a paper template by tracing round the hanger, adding at least 5 cm (2 in) all round. Cut two pieces of calico using the template as a guide.

By hand, sew the cream braid in a scroll design on to the right side of one of the calico pieces. Place the piece in an embroidery hoop or frame, and using several strands of embroidery thread and a large decorative stitch such as a chain stitch, embroider along the scroll design, following the curves of the braid. With one or two strands of embroidery thread, embroider a few small circles at random all over the calico piece. Move the embroidery hoop along as you work.

Now put the calico pieces with right sides together, and sew along the bottom edges, and a little way up the sides and along the top edge. Turn right-way out and press the seams. Cut strips of wadding to cover the hanger, and fairly

tightly wrap them round the hanger. Slip a small piece of cotton wool which has been impregnated with essential oil in among the wadding. Sew the wadding in place on the hanger around the top and bottom edges.

Now wind a length of cotton tape round the metal hook of the hanger, starting at the bottom, and working up and back down again. Sew the ends in place. Slip the hanger into the calico cover. Sew the top edge neatly together by hand, using a tiny hidden stitch. Sew a short length of cream ribbon to the base of the hanger hook, and gently thread the blue ribbon through the cream ribbon. Tie the blue ribbon in a big bow.

ABOVE A lovely embroidered hanger is ideal for special silk clothes and it is a gift which will last indefinitely.

GIFTS FOR THE KITCHEN

Delicious home-made food is difficult to resist, whether it is luxurious chocolate confections or useful storecupboard preserves. Making food gifts is rewarding and fun for the giver and shows time and thought contributed to the gift. You can also always multiply the quantities for the food gifts in this chapter, in order to make large amounts at one time and give the gifts to several different people. Along with food ideas, decorations and accessories for the kitchen are also included in this chapter, for those who would rather not be tempted by spiced nuts or Turkish Delight.

Give kitchen gifts in sensible re-usable containers where possible, so once the nuts have been nibbled or the herb paste finished there is still something to keep. Chocolates and sweets can be packaged every bit as beautifully as the best chocolatier would do if you take trouble to find little paper petit four cases, shredded tissue, really thick and crunchy cellophane and lovely covered boxes. Label anything which needs an explanation or provide a list of ingredients the way a commercial manufacturer does, so it is clear how the gift should be used. Explain too if a food item should be kept in a refrigerator or eaten quickly. If you give a home-made drink or liqueur, include a beautiful antique drinking glass, or if you give sweets, package a collection of the little delicacies on a lovely old china plate over-wrapped in cellophane.

Herb Mixes

Fresh herbs can be made into delicious pastes and pestos, and potted up into small jars. A spoonful of the mixture can transform a soup or casserole or make a pasta sauce of great style. Experimenting with new combinations, such as parsley and ground walnuts or coriander and green chilli, will produce your own unique blends. The traditional basil pesto with basil, pine nuts, parmesan, olive oil and garlic can also be made with the following method.

FRESH HERB OF YOUR CHOICE, SUCH AS PARSLEY, CORIANDER, MARJORAM, BASIL, CHIVES, CHERVIL AND SORREL

~

SALT

~

OLIVE OIL OR TASTELESS VEGETABLE OIL OF YOUR CHOICE

~

SMALL GLASS JARS

Strip the leaves of the herb from the stem very carefully and place them in a liquidiser or a food processor. Alternatively, place them in a pestle and mortar and grind the herbs.

Process the leaves until they are chopped quite finely. Add a pinch of salt, then drizzle in a little oil and process again. Continue adding oil until you have a thick herb paste.

Spoon the mixture into small jars, and pour a thin layer of clean oil over the top to completely cover the herb. Cork the jar or close tightly with a screw-top lid, and refrigerate. Eat within a week.

RIGHT Herb pastes make useful little presents for a cook. Remember to label the jars carefully, as the pastes look very similar.

Mulled Wine Spice Bags

Mulled wine is an old-fashioned warming drink for a cold winter's night. There are many versions of slightly sweetened and spiced red wine from all round the world. Best served from a large punch bowl or the saucepan it was heated in, mulled wine is very much a drink for entertaining a crowd. The spices for the drink are wrapped up in little muslin spicing bags, and the recipe below makes enough mixture to fill at least ten small bags.

10 CINNAMON STICKS
~
125 G (4 OUNCES) DRIED ORANGE PEEL
~
125 G (4 OUNCES) BLADE MACE
~
125 G (4 OUNCES) WHOLE CLOVES
~
125 G (4 OUNCES) WHOLE CORIANDER SEEDS
~
50 G (2 OUNCES) WHOLE ALLSPICE
~
10 WHOLE CARDAMOM PODS
~
10-12 SMALL MUSLIN SQUARES, MEASURING 12.5 CM
(5 IN) SQUARE
~
STRING
~
LABEL

Break or cut the cinnamon sticks into small pieces. Snip the orange peel if it is too big. Put all the spices into a bowl. Stir thoroughly to combine, then place a spoonful of spice mixture into a square of muslin. Pull the edges together and tie with string.

Pack the little bags into a small wooden box and label well. Give a recipe for mulled wine and suggest other uses for the bags, such as using them to flavour dried or fresh fruit compotes, fruit jellies and jams, or even to fill the house with a delicious scent by simmering them in a pan of water with the lid off.

RIGHT A selection of mulled wine spice bags packed into a box with cinnamon and some of the other spices makes a festive Christmas gift.

Mulled Wine Recipe

Include this recipe with the mulled wine spice bags, left, if you are presenting the sachets as a gift.

1 BOTTLE RED WINE
~
1 MULLED WINE SPICE BAG
~
30 ML (2 TABLESPOONS) SUGAR
~
FRESH LEMON OR ORANGE PEEL

Pour the wine into a large saucepan, and warm over a low heat. Add the spice bag and sugar. When the sugar has dissolved, taste and add more sugar if necessary. Add the fresh lemon or orange peel. Bring the wine slowly up to the boil, then take it off the heat immediately. Leave to infuse for a few minutes, then serve.

Flower-flavoured Liqueur

~

Drinks have been flavoured with flowers and herbs for centuries and there are many unusual variations. This slightly perfumed drink should be sipped after a meal. Once you have made this version, you can try experimenting and creating different liqueurs. Using tarragon and other herbs will give a flavour a little like Chartreuse, or you could try a single flower scent, such as rose or violet. Eau de vie can be used in place of vodka, but it is not always easy to obtain. You could also make it with brandy, which would give the drink a different character.

1 CUP DRIED ORANGE BLOSSOM,
AVAILABLE FROM
A HERBALIST
~
1/2 CUP DRIED LEMON VERBENA LEAVES
OR 1/4 CUP FRESH
~
1 STICK CINNAMON
~
4 CLOVES

ABOVE This orange blossom and cinnamon liqueur is best served with sweet almond biscuits after a meal. Include some biscuits with the liqueur as a gift.

1 UNWAXED SMALL ORANGE, SCRUBBED CLEAN
~
1 BOTTLE VODKA
~
SUGAR SYRUP
~
PAPER FILTER, SUCH AS A COFFEE FILTER
~
DECORATIVE BOTTLE WITH SEALABLE TOP

Place the orange blossom, lemon verbena and cinnamon in a large, wide-necked glass jar with a sealable lid. Stick the cloves into the orange and add this to the jar. Pour the vodka over and leave for six weeks.

Strain the vodka off the fruit and other ingredients. Using a paper filter, pour the liquid through the filter into a clean bowl, and sweeten to taste with sugar syrup. Pour the liqueur into a decorative bottle with a cork or sealable top, and label.

Flavoured Vinegars
~

All types of flavourings can be found to create completely original and tasty preserves. Some of the simplest flavours and scents work best of all. You may like to try tarragon, lavender, elderflower, mint or rose petals. Or use a combination, such as garlic and ginger root or cardamom and orange. Experiment with fruit as well; sour red cherries with a few spices makes a delicious vinegar and a pickled fruit at the same time. Choose your own combination of flowers, herbs and spices for this recipe, and adapt the measurements to the quantity you prefer.

600 ML (1 PINT) WHITE WINE OR CIDER VINEGAR
~
1 CUP FRESH FLOWERS, HERBS OR SPICES

Some recipes suggest heating the vinegar first, but it is not necessary if you use plenty of flavouring. Put the flowers, herbs or spices into a sealable wide-necked glass jar. Pour over the vinegar, tightly close the jar, and leave in a warm place for several days or up to two weeks.

Strain the vinegar off the ingredients and re-bottle the vinegar with a few fresh petals or herbs.

If you want to make rose petal vinegar, add a small proportion of red wine vinegar to boost the pretty pink colouring. Use highly scented red or deep pink petals and leave them in the vinegar until they have lost their colour, which may take several weeks.

ABOVE *Scented oils and vinegars make excellent storecupboard standbys. Include a label describing the ingredients and suggesting uses for the oil or vinegar if you are giving it as a gift.*

Flavoured Oils
~

Create an oil to your taste and according to its final use. If the oil is to be used for dressing salads and vegetables, then use a well-flavoured oil, such as olive oil. If it is to be used for stir-frying, than choose a neutral groundnut or sunflower oil. If the flavourings are very strong, such as chilli or ginger, use a bland oil.

600 ML (1 PINT) OIL OF YOUR CHOICE
~
1 CUP FRESH FLOWERS, HERBS OR SPICES

The method for making flavoured oils is similar to that of vinegars. Simply add the flavourings you are using to a sealable wide-necked glass jar and pour in the oil. Tightly close the lid and leave in a warm place for several days.

You do not normally need to strain off the liquid before re-bottling, but you may like to do so and add a fresh ingredient to the oil. If you make citrus oil, coil a long narrow strip of fresh lemon peel into the bottle when re-bottling. Insert a pretty dried red chilli in a bottle of chilli oil. Use within one week.

Scented Sugars

~

Scented sugars are rather luxurious ingredients for the store-cupboard, but excellent as a gift as they are difficult to find in a food shop. The delicate sugars can be used to flavour biscuits, meringues, cakes, sauces and ice creams. A small spoonful stirred into cream, yoghurt or fromage frais makes an unusual and delicious sauce for a pudding. Place the finished sugar in a pretty or unusual glass jar.

250 G (9 OUNCES) CASTER SUGAR

~

1/2 CUP DRIED ROSE PETALS OR DRIED CITRUS PEEL, OR 1/4 CUP DRIED LAVENDER

~

DECORATIVE GLASS JARS

To make the sugars, you need to pulverise the dried flavour-ings before adding them to the sugar. If you grind the flavourings with the sugar you will make powdered sugar.

Grind the rose petals, lavender or dried peels in a very clean coffee mill, or a food processor or liquidiser. Grind until the ingredients are small pieces, but stop before they become a powder. Combine the ingredients with the sugar, stirring thoroughly, and place the scented sugar in a decorative container.

If you are making lemon or orange sugar, you can easily dry the citrus peel yourself. Remove the skin from unwaxed and, preferably, organically grown fruits, then leave the peel in a warm and airy place until dried.

BELOW Rose petal and lavender sugars are faintly flower scented and look beautiful. They make a lovely gift for someone who loves to bake sweets and desserts.

Candied Cardamom Nuts

These sweet nuts should be eaten soon after they are made, and should be labelled accordingly if giving them as a gift. Use either walnuts or pecans for this recipe.

125 G (4 OUNCES) WALNUT OR PECAN HALVES
~
JUICE OF ONE ORANGE MADE UP TO 150 ML
(¼ PINT) WITH WATER
~
225 G (8 OUNCES) GRANULATED SUGAR
~
GRATED PEEL OF ONE ORANGE
~
10 ML (2 TEASPOONS) GROUND CARDAMOM, GROUND
BY HAND IF POSSIBLE

Preheat the oven to 180°C (350°F, Gas mark 4). Spread the nuts evenly on a baking sheet and place in the oven to heat through for 15 minutes.

Meanwhile put the orange juice and water mixture in a heavy-based saucepan, and add the sugar. Dissolve over very low heat, then bring to the boil. Cook rapidly without stirring until the temperature reaches 116°C (234°F), the soft ball stage, on a sugar thermometer.

Remove the pan from the heat, and add the orange rind, cardamom and nuts. Stir vigorously with a wooden spoon until the mixture turns creamy. Turn out on to a shallow plate and separate the walnuts or pecans before they set. Store the nuts in an airtight container. The recipe makes about 250 g (9 ounces), enough for four people as a snack.

BELOW Pack the savoury or candied spiced nuts in twists of thick cellophane tied with a satin or velvet ribbon for a pretty packaged look.

Savoury Spiced Nuts

Simple nuts can be transformed by spicy flavourings. They should be eaten soon after they are made, so always label them accordingly. Buy nuts as fresh as possible; if in doubt buy them in their shells and shell them yourself. Nuts can become stale quickly, so start with the best ingredients you can buy. Pecans, walnuts, almonds, brazil nuts and hazelnuts all work well with this recipe.

250 G (9 OUNCES) ALMONDS, PECANS,
WALNUTS OR A MIXTURE
~
60 ML (4 TABLESPOONS)
FINE SEA SALT
~
BUTTER
~
SUNFLOWER OR
GROUNDNUT OIL
~
2.5 ML (½ TEASPOON) GROUND CUMIN
~
1.25 ML (¼ TEASPOON) CHILLI POWDER

ABOVE Spiced nuts can also be displayed in metal baskets, as here. If you are giving them as a gift, wrap the baskets in cellophane to keep the nuts fresh. Wooden or card boxes can also be used, but do line them with foil or cellophane to protect the box.

2.5 ML (½ TEASPOON) PAPRIKA
~
2.5 ML (½ TEASPOON) READY-MADE CURRY SPICE
BLEND

Preheat the oven to 150°C (300°F, Gas mark 2). Liberally butter a low-sided baking tray, and cover it with nuts one-layer deep. Drizzle over some oil so the nuts are lightly moistened, then place the tray in the low oven for 50 minutes. Check them occasionally, and stir.

Remove from the oven, and pour the nuts into a large bowl, adding the salt and spices. Mix very thoroughly and leave covered for a couple of hours or longer. Shake off the excess salt. Store the nuts in an airtight container, or package as a gift. The recipe makes about 250 g (9 ounces).

Rose Turkish Delight

This is made by a fairly easy and quick method. Some Middle Eastern versions need cooking for three hours, plus exotic ingredients. The packaging of the finished product is most important. Try to find small, round wooden boxes or use card boxes. Crumple waxed paper inside to hold the sweets, and cut a circle of paper to cover them before putting on the lid. You could also make Creme de Menthe-flavoured jellies in the same way, using a little green natural colouring and 6 drops of peppermint oil.

60 ML (4 TABLESPOONS) TRIPLE-DISTILLED
ROSEWATER
~
30 ML (2 TABLESPOONS) POWDERED GELATINE
~
450 G (16 OUNCES) GRANULATED WHITE SUGAR
~
150 ML (¼ PINT) WATER
~
MUSLIN SQUARE
~
10 DROPS ROSE OR ROSE GERANIUM ESSENTIAL OIL
~
FEW DROPS NATURAL PINK COLOURING
~
25 G (1 OUNCE) CORNFLOUR, FOR DUSTING
~
50 G (2 OUNCES) ICING SUGAR, FOR DUSTING

Pour the rosewater into a small cup and sprinkle on the gelatine. Leave to soak.

Measure the sugar and water into a saucepan, and dissolve the sugar over a very low heat. Strain through muslin into a clean pan and bring back to the boil. Boil rapidly without stirring until it reaches 116°C (234°F), the soft ball stage, on a sugar thermometer. Remove from the heat and add the gelatine. Return to a very low heat and stir for just a minute to mix in the gelatine.

Remove from the heat and add the food colouring and rose or rose geranium essential oil. Pour the syrup into an 18cm (7in) square oiled tin and leave to solidify to a jelly. Sift the cornflour and icing sugar together on to a sheet of non-stick paper. Lift a corner of the jelly, and pull it out of the tin on to the sugar mixture. Cut into squares and toss them all in the sugar. Makes about 18 squares.

To make Lemon Turkish Delight, use orange flower water in place of rosewater, and the juice of one lemon in place of 30 ml (2 tablespoons) of the water in recipe. Use a very little yellow natural colouring in place of pink, and flavour with 6 drops of lemon oil in place of the rose.

BELOW Rose Turkish Delight makes a pretty gift when wrapped in crumpled white paper in a round wooden box.

Chocolate Violet Truffles

~

Although calorific, these rich chocolate truffles are absolutely heavenly. You can make larger or smaller quantities of the recipe if you wish, but do not economise on the ingredients. You must use very high quality dark chocolate and fresh cream. If you have a problem finding violet liqueur, substitute brandy and add crushed crystallised violets to the truffle mixture.

500 G (1 POUND 2 OUNCES) PLAIN CHOCOLATE, AT LEAST 60% COCOA SOLIDS

~

300 ML (½ PINT) FRESH CREAM

~

A MINIATURE BOTTLE OF VIOLET LIQUEUR, AVAILABLE FROM SPECIALIST WINE MERCHANTS

~

250 G (9 OUNCES) PLAIN CHOCOLATE, TO COAT

~

CRYSTALLISED VIOLET PETALS

ABOVE Gold petit four cases set off the dark colouring of these hand-crafted chocolate truffles and make a gift that looks like it was bought from a professional chocolatier.

Melt the chocolate and cream together in a double-saucepan until soft enough to stir and combine completely. Add 15 ml (1 tablespoon) of liqueur and stir. Pour the mixture into a tin lined with non-stick paper. When cool and almost firm, spoon out small pieces of the chocolate mixture and, with your hands, quickly shape into small rough balls. Chill the truffles to harden.

Melt the coating chocolate in a double-saucepan. Spear each truffle with a small fork and dip into the melted chocolate. Leave on a piece of marble or non-stick paper to cool, scattering crystallised violet petals over each truffle before the chocolate sets. Makes about 30 truffles.

Herb Posies

Dried flowers and herbs are an excellent way to bring colour and prettiness to the kitchen, a room that has become the centre of the household and a place in which to spend time. These three versions of a Victorian posy have lavender, roses and marjoram included in them, and show that dried flowers do not have to be dull and colourless.

Rose and Marjoram Posy

20 SMALL DRIED RED ROSES
~
7 MEDIUM-SIZE DRIED PINK ROSES
~
1 BUNCH DRIED MARJORAM
~
WIRE

Hold a red rose as the central flower, and surround this with the pink roses. Wire the stems tightly in place. Now add a ring of the dried marjoram round the pink roses, and wire the stems together again. Finish with a ring of red roses round the outside. Tie stems together and trim the ends of the stems to the same length.

Hyssop, Hydrangea and Red Rose Posy

1 BUNCH DRIED HYSSOP
~
12 DRIED RED ROSES
~
1 BUNCH DRIED BLUE HYDRANGEA
~
WIRE

Hold a small bunch of hyssop in your hand as the central flowers, then ring it with the red roses. Stop and tie the stems with wire if the posy gets difficult to handle as you go. Finally make a wide band of hydrangea round the roses. Tightly tie the stems again with wire and trim all the stems to the same length.

Marigold, Yellow Rose and Lavender Posy

15 DRIED YELLOW ROSES
~
1 BUNCH DEEP PURPLE DRIED LAVENDER
~
15 DRIED YELLOW AFRICAN MARIGOLDS
~
WIRE

Gather the yellow roses together in your hands, making a round bunch. Circle this with a ring of lavender and tightly tie the stems together with wire. Make a ring of marigolds round the lavender, and tie the stems together again with wire. Trim all the ends of the stems to the same length.

LEFT AND BELOW Dried flowers are combined with dried herbs to create colourful posies for kitchen decorations.

Bay Leaf Balls

~

Little sculptural shapes wrapped in leaves have become popular decorations. All kinds of shapes can be cut from foam bases and covered in fresh or dried leaves. The leaves can be glued into place or pinned with decorative pins, tacks or studs. Fresh bay leaves look wonderfully glossy and green and are delightfully aromatic when handled. They will gently and attractively fade and dry on the balls.

POLYSTYRENE, COTTON OR FOAM BALL SHAPES

~

LARGE QUANTITY FRESH BAY LEAVES

~

BRASS PINS, UPHOLSTERY TACKS OR SMALL NAILS

ABOVE Tiny brass pins are used on this bay leaf ball in the foreground. Pile several of these balls into a bowl for a fragrant arrangement, or simply place one ball somewhere it can be admired and its culinary aroma enjoyed.

Sort out leaves which are all roughly the same size and shape. This will make covering the ball easier than using varied sizes of leaf. You can either work neatly and systematically, placing the leaves in rows, or in a more random fashion, criss-crossing the leaves in all directions. For the neater version, pin the leaves only at the top and bottom of each leaf. For the random method, pin the leaves where necessary to hold the leaves secure.

Mug Warmer

The mug warmer is a great way to add fragrance to everyday experiences. The padded warmer fits around a mug and the scent is released by the heat of the liquid in the mug. You may like to choose essential oils according to your favourite hot drink, such as cinnamon for hot chocolate or orange for herbal teas.

COTTON FABRIC
~
THIN SYNTHETIC SHEET WADDING
~
SEWING THREAD
~
COTTON WOOL
~
ESSENTIAL OILS, SUCH AS CINNAMON, CORIANDER
OR ORANGE
~
RIBBON OR PRESS STUDS

ABOVE A pair of these mug warmers makes a wonderful Christmas gift for those who love a hot drink on a cold winter's evening.

Cut one piece of fabric 42 x 26 cm (16½ x 10 in) and two pieces of wadding 39 x 11.5 cm (15½ x 4½ in). Fold the fabric in half lengthwise with right sides together, and sew round one short side and the long side. Turn right sides out and press seams.

Insert the two thin sheets of wadding. Scent a piece of cotton wool with a few drops of essential oil, and tuck this in between the two sheets of wadding. Sew up the final short edge by hand, using a tiny hidden stitch. Sew a short length of ribbon to each short edge of the mug warmer to tie the warmer on to the mug, or attach press studs at the short edges.

Spice Mixture
~

Use this mixture to fill the spice-filled mat below. You may like to adapt the ingredients according to what you have available. Choose any quantity of the spices you desire, adjusting according to how the mixture smells to you.

DRIED ORANGE AND LEMON PEEL
~
BROKEN CINNAMON STICKS
~
CLOVES
~
CORIANDER SEEDS
~
BRUISED DRIED GINGER ROOT
~
STAR ANISE
~
A LITTLE ORRIS ROOT POWDER

Mix all the ingredients together, stirring thoroughly. Store in an airtight container, and use as required.

ABOVE This hot plate mat is filled with a mixture of cinnamon, cloves and ginger, along with other highly fragrant herbs. The mat makes an ideal gift for someone with a new home, and brings extra scent into the kitchen.

Spice-filled Mat
~

This lovely idea is quite simple to make. Ready-made place mats have been used as the basis for the padded mat to utilize the attractive border pattern. The size is perfect for a large plate or casserole dish. Of course you could use any fabric and size of mat accordingly. A sachet filled with a spice mixture fits inside the mat, so it can be removed for laundering.

LOOSE-WOVEN COTTON FABRIC
~
1 READY-MADE COTTON PLACE MAT
~
COTTON FABRIC FOR THE BACKING IN A COLOUR COMPLEMENTARY TO THE PLACE MAT
~
SYNTHETIC WADDING IN A SHEET
~
WIDE COTTON BINDING
~
SEWING THREAD
~
SPICE MIXTURE (SEE ABOVE)

First make an inner sachet for the spice. Measure the place mat and cut the loose-woven cotton about 4 cm (1 1/2 in) smaller all round than the place mat. With right sides together, sew around three edges. Turn right-sides out and loosely fill the sachet with spice mixture. Sew the fourth side closed by hand.

Cut a sheet of wadding the same size as the place mat. Cut the cotton backing fabric the same size as top mat but add 14 cm (5 1/2 in) more to the width.

Now cut the backing fabric in half along its length and fold under the two cut edges by 2 cm (3/4 in) and hem in place. Press.

On a flat work surface, position the two pieces of backing fabric with hemmed edges overlapping each other 5 cm (2 in) and the wrong sides of the backing fabric facing upwards. Check the backing piece is exactly the same size as the place mat and wadding, and adjust overlap if necessary. Loosely tack the overlap seam to hold the two backing pieces together.

On top of the wrong-sides of the backing fabric, place the wadding, then the place mat, right-sides facing upwards. You should now have a layer of wadding sandwiched between the backing and the place mat. Pin the cotton tape all round the edges and sew on, through all three thicknesses. Remove the tacking on the backing fabric. Slip the sachet in through the open slit at the back.

BEAUTY AND HEALTH GIFTS

Few people attempt to make their own versions of cosmetics and beauty products, imagining it is difficult or needs special equipment. Neither is the case, and it is actually very rewarding to create wholesome luxuries for the skin or bath that you can tailor-make to your requirements. You have control over all the ingredients and you can scent the products as you like. There is no great mystique to making colognes and eau de toilettes, and it is even simpler to make wonderfully aromatic massage oils. The ingredients which you will need are generally easy to find. Local chemists have many of the necessary items at an often cheaper price than at specialist herbalist's shops. If you do not see what you need on view, ask the pharmacist, as items can be ordered specially or they may be stored out of view. Buying oils in bulk in plain bottles often makes them much less expensive than small amounts in fancy packaging.

Look for suitable containers for the products you make. Although you can buy new empty glass bottles and jars, recycling old ones you have at home is more creative and cost-efficient. You can even use jars meant for totally different purposes, and transform them with your own labels or decorate them with cut-out paper shapes. Always label or include a note with the gift, to explain exactly what the product is and how it should be used.

Scented Sea Shells and Pebbles

This idea is exceedingly simple, but the results are both pretty and fragrant. You will need all types of shells and marine pebbles. Small bags of mixed shells or single large or unusual shells can be bought from specialist or beachfront shops, but you may like to collect shells and pebbles from beaches and riversides yourself.

MIXED SHELLS, PEBBLES AND OTHER SHORE FINDS
~
ESSENTIAL OILS, SCENTING OILS OR ROOM PERFUMES
~
CONTAINERS, SUCH AS GLASS JARS, PLATES AND SHALLOW BOWLS

Small stones and sea-washed pebbles add different colours and textures. They absorb the scenting oils if they have been rubbed and are slightly porous on their surface. Even very hard and seemingly impervious materials hold scent for quite a long time.

Choose a fresh or lightly floral fragrance. There are some wonderful room perfumes with an outdoor, marine smell which would be perfect. Simply drop a little scenting oil or room-scenter oil on the shell or pebble. If you can only find a spray form of the scent you desire, then spray the shells and pebbles heavily. The scent will be slightly absorbed into the objects and will last a couple of weeks, depending on the strength of the perfume. You will need to refresh the scent.

As a gift, fill a bag or box with the shells and pebbles, and a spare bottle of scenting oil or perfume. Or you may like to display the objects in a glass jar, shallow bowl or plate, and wrap with cellophane. Avoid rustic baskets as containers for a beach collection, unless they are bleached and weathered or painted in pale blues, greys and whites.

RIGHT A marine collection of scented shells and pebbles are best displayed in glass jars and plates, so their pale colours can be appreciated without distraction.

Relaxing Bath Mix

A long and luxurious bath is still an important ritual, and helps relieve stress. In addition to adding fragrance to the bath, this mixture contains soothing herbs to help relax the mind and body; the herbs and oils are beneficial to the skin, too.

1 LITRE (1¾ PINTS) STILL MINERAL WATER
~
50 G (2 OUNCES) RICE FLOUR
~
100 ML (7 TABLESPOONS) CLEAR HONEY, SUCH AS ACACIA
~
40 G (1½ OUNCE) DRIED CHAMOMILE FLOWERS
~
30 G (1¼ OUNCE) DRIED RED ROSE PETALS
~
20 G (¾ OUNCE) DRIED VALERIAN ROOT
~
LARGE MUSLIN SQUARE
~
10 ML (2 TEASPOONS) SWEET ALMOND OIL
~
150 ML (¼ PINT) ROSEWATER
~
15 DROPS CHAMOMILE ESSENTIAL OIL
~
15 DROPS ROSE GERANIUM OR ROSE ESSENTIAL OIL
~
DECORATIVE BOTTLE AND LABEL

ABOVE This luxurious bath liquid is scented with chamomile and rose to aid in relaxing and soothing the body. It is best for a pre-bedtime soak, when it can be used to induce a lovely feeling of drowsiness.

Put the water and rice flour in a stainless steel pan and bring to the boil, stirring well. Then add the honey and stir until dissolved. Add the dried herbs, stir again, and remove from the heat. Leave mixture to cool.

When cool, strain the mixture through a large piece of muslin and discard the soaked herbs. Add the almond oil and rosewater to the mixture and stir. Finally add the essential oils, stir very well, and bottle into a clean dry glass bottle.

Attach a hand-written label, suggesting a spoonful or two to be used for each bath. Explain that the bottle should be shaken well before using, and the spoonfuls should be poured in the bath under the tap.

Invigorating Bath Gel

Designed to energise and invigorate, this bath gel is ideal for a morning bath. If you do not have all the different herbs, use those you have available or try substituting others. The herbs selected should have a brisk and fresh scent. The herb infusion is a pale yellowish brown in colour, and not terribly pretty. You could colour the mixture slightly by adding a few drops of natural food colouring to make a pale blue or greenish blue gel.

450 ML (3/4 PINT) STILL MINERAL WATER
~
10 G (1/4 OUNCE) EACH OF DRIED ROSEMARY, LAVENDER, ANGELICA, LEMON VERBENA, SAGE, PEPPERMINT, BLACKBERRY LEAVES AND COMFREY
~
45 ML (3 TABLESPOONS) GLYCERINE
~
30 ML (2 TABLESPOONS) WITCH HAZEL
~
6 DROPS LEMON VERBENA ESSENTIAL OIL
~
3 DROPS EUCALYPTUS ESSENTIAL OIL
~
3 DROPS PINE ESSENTIAL OIL
~
3 DROPS LAVENDER ESSENTIAL OIL
~
3 DROPS CYPRESS ESSENTIAL OIL
~
LARGE MUSLIN SQUARE
~
120 ML (8 TABLESPOONS) GRATED PURE UNPERFUMED SOAP (CASTILE)
30 ML (2 TABLESPOONS) POWDERED GELATINE
~
2-3 DROPS NATURAL BLUE OR GREEN FOOD COLOURING, OPTIONAL
~
DECORATIVE BOTTLES

Boil the still mineral water. Place all the dried herbs in a bowl and pour over the boiling water. Stir well, and leave to infuse. Stir occasionally until the mixture cools. Meanwhile, mix together the glycerine, witch hazel and essential oils.

Strain the herb infusion through muslin, discarding the herbs, and re-heat the liquid in an old saucepan. Dissolve the grated soap in the heated liquid. When dissolved, combine the liquid with the essential oil mixture. Whisk together well and add the gelatine. Add the colouring, if desired, whisking continuously until all the ingredients are completely combined.

Check the fragrance and adjust by adding more essential oils if necessary. The gel will be very dilute in the bath so the fragrance should be powerful. Pour the mixture into small, clean and dry bottles. Use a small amount in a bath, adding it under the running tap for maximum froth.

LEFT This herbal bath gel combines dried herbs and essential oils for their refreshing scent and invigorating properties.

Old-fashioned Lavender Water

A lovely refreshing cologne, lavender water is useful to have in supply and can be used lavishly. Lavender is used for its scent, but it is also a healing herb used in its concentrated form to help skin recover after burns or wounds. For the best results, use fresh lavender flowers picked when they are just fully open on a dry sunny day. This is when they have the maximum volatile oil available. Dried flowers can be used but they need to be made into an infusion first.

1 CUP FRESH LAVENDER FLOWERS, STRIPPED FROM THEIR STALKS
~
WIDE-NECKED GLASS JAR
~
1 LITRE (1 ³/₄ PINTS) VODKA
~
¹/₂ LITRE (18 FLUID OUNCES) SPRING WATER
~
MUSLIN SQUARE
~
10 DROPS LAVENDER ESSENTIAL OIL
~
FILTER PAPER, SUCH AS A COFFEE FILTER
~
DECORATIVE BOTTLES

ABOVE Lavender water has a clean fresh scent, making a light perfume as well as a refreshing cologne and insect-repellant.

Place the lavender flowers in a wide-necked jar with an airtight lid. Pour the vodka over the lavender, and close the lid tightly. Leave in a warm sunny place, such as a windowsill. Shake the jar once or twice a day for three weeks.

Strain the liquid from the lavender through the muslin. Add the spring water and the drops of essential oil. Pour the liquid back into the jar, and leave for another week, again shaking the jar daily. Finally strain the liquid through filter paper until it is as clear as possible, and pour into decorative bottles.

If you are using dried flowers, first boil the spring water and pour over the dried lavender to infuse. Then strain and combine the liquid with the vodka and essential oils, and proceed as described in the instructions above.

To use, splash the lavender water on the skin when you are hot or tired. You can also use the lavender water as a mild insect-repellant during warm summer evenings.

Rosewater and Glycerine

~

This old-fashioned cosmetic has a very mild toning effect on all kinds of skin types. It is gentle and unlikely to upset sensitive skin conditions. Rosewater can be bought from chemists or herbalists and is a slightly scented but colourless liquid. There is no need to buy triple-distilled rosewater for this recipe, just the ordinary kind.

120 ML (8 TABLESPOONS) ROSEWATER
~
90 ML (6 TABLESPOONS) WITCH HAZEL
~
45 ML (3 TABLESPOONS) GLYCERINE
~
NATURAL RED FOOD COLOURING, OPTIONAL
~
DECORATIVE BOTTLES

ABOVE This delicate blend of rosewater and glycerine has a light rose fragrance and is suitable for the most sensitive skin types.

Mix all the rosewater, witch hazel and glycerine together very thoroughly, whisking them well until combined. The result is a clear liquid, which could then be coloured very slightly with a few drops of natural food colour. Purists might not approve, but only a very small amount needs to be added to give the palest pink blush tinge. Pour the liquid into small decorative bottles, and close tightly with a cork or screw-top lid.

Use small quantities of this mixture after cleansing the skin with a cream cleanser or after washing. Or, use any time as a refreshing and quick tonic for the skin.

Orange and Coriander Cologne

This fruity-scented cologne can be used to splash on the skin after bathing or as a light perfume. The cologne is quite warm and spicy in its fragrance, and would suit men or women. As you add essential oils, adjust the proportions as your nose persuades you. Store any colognes you make in tightly sealed and stoppered bottles, and preferably out of strong light, to preserve the fragrance.

15 ML (1 TABLESPOON) CORIANDER SEEDS
~
WIDE-NECKED JAR
~
PEEL OF 2 FRESH ORANGES
~
200 ML (⅓ PINT) VODKA
~
MUSLIN SQUARE, DOUBLED
~
10 DROPS ORANGE ESSENTIAL OIL
~
10 DROPS BERGAMOT ESSENTIAL OIL
~
5 DROPS CINNAMON ESSENTIAL OIL
~
5 DROPS NEROLI ESSENTIAL OIL

ABOVE *The spicy-scented Orange and Coriander Cologne has a scent that will appeal to both men and women.*

90 ML (6 TABLESPOONS) SPRING WATER
~
PAPER FILTER, SUCH AS A COFFEE FILTER
~
DECORATIVE BOTTLES

Crush the coriander seeds with a pestle and mortar, and put them into a wide-necked jar. Add the peel from the oranges, and pour the vodka over. Stir very well and close the lid tightly. Leave for a week, stirring or shaking daily.

After a week, strain through a doubled piece of muslin. Then add the drops of essential oil, stirring again for two minutes or so to disperse the different oils. Transfer to the jar and tightly close the lid. Leave for 48 hours, then add the spring water, again stirring very well for a few minutes. Leave for up to four weeks, if you can, as the fragrance matures and mellows with time. If you do not have a month to spare, leave for 48 hours.

Strain the liquid through a paper filter several times, and finally bottle into attractive containers.

Rose and Vanilla Cologne

The wonderful scent of roses with the warm hint of vanilla and cardamom makes a sweet-scented cologne. Pure rose essential oil is very expensive, but some extra rose fragrance is required to boost the fragrance of the fresh petals. You can substitute rose geranium oil in place of true rose, if you prefer.

2 CUPS FRESH HIGHLY SCENTED DEEP RED OR
PINK ROSE PETALS
~
WIDE-NECKED GLASS JAR
~
1 VANILLA POD
~
10 CARDAMOM PODS
~
200 ML (1/3 PINT) VODKA
~
MUSLIN SQUARE, DOUBLED
~
5 DROPS VANILLA ESSENTIAL OIL
~
10 DROPS ROSE ESSENTIAL OIL
~
5 DROPS ROMAN CHAMOMILE ESSENTIAL OIL
~
90 ML (6 TABLESPOONS) ROSEWATER

ABOVE The romantic floral fragrance of roses is combined with vanilla and cardamom in this Rose and Vanilla Cologne.

90 ML (6 TABLESPOONS) SPRING WATER
~
PAPER FILTER, SUCH AS A COFFEE FILTER
~
DECORATIVE BOTTLES

Place the rose petals in a wide-necked jar. Bruise the vanilla pod a little to expose the tiny seeds and add to the jar. Break open the cardamoms and add these to the jar. Pour over the vodka. Close the lid tightly, and leave for a week, shaking the jar daily.

Strain the liquid through doubled muslin. Add the essential oils and rosewater, and stir very well to combine. Leave for 48 hours. Then add the spring water and stir again. Transfer the liquid to the jar, tightly close, and leave for up to four weeks, shaking the jar occasionally.

Strain the cologne through filter paper a couple of times to remove any of the tiny vanilla seeds, and bottle into decorative containers.

Soothing Skin Salve

~

This hand-and-body cream is a little more robust than the Apricot and Marigold Hand Cream on page 73. It is ideal to use after hands have had rough treatment, especially due to gardening or decorating. Try to find shallow china or glass pots for the salve, as the surface area of the cream should be wide enough to allow a scooping out of the salve with the fingers. The lavender oil scents the cream and adds healing and soothing properties.

50 G (2 OUNCES) SWEET ALMOND OIL

~

20 G (³/₄ OUNCE) BLEACHED BEESWAX GRANULES

~

10 G (¹/₃ OUNCE) COCOA BUTTER

~

40 G (1 ¹/₂ OUNCE) ORANGE FLOWER WATER

ABOVE This pure lavender-scented skin salve is a robust moisturiser, best presented in a wide-necked porcelain jar.

10 DROPS LAVENDER ESSENTIAL OIL

~

SHALLOW WIDE-NECKED CERAMIC OR GLASS POTS

Melt the oil, wax and cocoa butter in a double-saucepan or in a bowl resting over a pan of simmering water. When it has melted, heat the orange flower water almost to boiling point. Add the orange flower water in small stages to the melted oils, whisking the mixture constantly, ideally with a small hand blender.

Add the lavender essential oil and stir in well. Pour the mixture into small shallow sterile pots.

Apricot and Marigold Hand Cream

Although especially useful for hands, this lotion is a good all-round skin moisturiser for dry skin anywhere on the body. The oils and waxes are melted, then an emulsion is created by slowly adding a non-oily ingredient, in this case an infusion of marigold. The mixture will turn white and thicken. You can add a very little natural colouring if the marigold infusion has not made the mixture pale yellow.

300 ML (1/2 PINT) SPRING WATER

1 CUP DRIED MARIGOLD PETALS OR 2 CUPS FRESH

60 ML (4 TABLESPOONS) APRICOT KERNEL OIL

25 ML (1 1/2 TABLESPOONS) COCONUT OIL

25 ML (1 1/2 TABLESPOONS) AVOCADO OIL

7.5 ML (1/2 TABLESPOON) BLEACHED BEESWAX GRANULES

2.5 ML (1/2 TEASPOON) BORAX POWDER

ESSENTIAL OIL OF YOUR CHOICE, SEE PAGE 94, OR PURE ALMOND ESSENCE

NATURAL ORANGE FOOD COLOURING, OPTIONAL

GLASS JARS OR BOTTLES

Boil the spring water and pour over the marigold petals. Stir vigorously, then leave the infusion until it is completely cold. Strain the liquid and discard the petals.

Place the apricot, coconut and avocado oils, with the beeswax, into a double-saucepan or a bowl resting over a saucepan of simmering water. Stir until the ingredients have dissolved. Meanwhile, dissolve the borax in 60 ml (4 tablespoons) of the marigold infusion.

When the oils are completely dissolved, pour the marigold-borax infusion into the oils, stirring constantly until you have a smooth creamy mixture. Stir in a drop or two of pure almond essence or a floral essential oil to give the cream a little perfume. You may also like to stir in a drop of orange food colouring for a pretty pale apricot-coloured cream.

Pour the mixture into small, sterile jars or bottles with tight-fitting corks or screw-top lids, and close tightly. The cream should be kept very cool to prolong its life.

ABOVE Apricot and Marigold Hand Cream is a light moisturiser for dry skin, and has been elegantly presented here in a decorative bottle with a gold bow.

Scented Massage Oil

~

The base oil for this massage oil acts as a carrier for perfume, as it has no scent of its own. You can experiment with essential oils to create all kinds of blends. For a soothing and relaxing massage oil, use essential oils such as: benzoin, cedarwood, chamomile, clary sage, geranium, lavender, marjoram, melissa, neroli, rose, sage, sandalwood or ylang ylang. For an invigorating massage, use essential oils such as: basil, bergamot, cinnamon, clove, ginger, jasmine, juniper, orange, peppermint, rosemary or thyme.

300 ML (½ PINT) SWEET ALMOND, SAFFLOWER,
APRICOT OR PEACH KERNEL OIL
~
10 ML (2 TEASPOONS) ESSENTIAL OILS TO PERFUME,
SEE ABOVE AND PAGE 94
~
GLASS BOTTLE OR JAR WITH A SCREW-TOP LID
~
DECORATIVE BOTTLES

ABOVE Include a label with the massage oil, explaining whether it is a relaxing or an invigorating oil. Ideally, accompany the gift with a manual on massage.

The oil used as the base carrier for the perfume should be pure and of good quality. Choose one single essential oil or use several different oils for a blended scent.

To mix the oils together, use a bottle which has a larger capacity than you need. Pour in the base oil, then add the essential oil. Close the lid tightly. Twist, turn and gently shake the bottle so the oils mix together. Pour the massage oil into pretty decorative bottles.

When making this oil, you can make up quite large quantities if you like. You must, however, never exceed 1 drop of essential oil for every 1 ml base oil, or 5 drops of essential oil for every 1 teaspoon of base oil. Also useful to know is that 20 drops of essential oil is equal to 1 ml and 100 drops are equal to 1 teaspoon.

Rose and Mint Body Scrub

A big jar of this body scrub is great to have in supply beside the bath or shower. The grains work on the skin, gently exfoliating and softening it. Here the jar used is an antique apothecary's jar which has been decorated with a Victorian scrap cut-out of roses simply glued to the outside of the jar. The measurements given below allow you to easily adapt the quantity as you desire.

1 MEASURE FINE OATMEAL
~
1 MEASURE FRESHLY GROUND
UNBLANCHED ALMONDS
~
1/2 MEASURE DRIED
MILK POWDER
~
1/2 MEASURE WHEAT BRAN
~
2 MEASURES DRIED SCENTED
ROSE PETALS
~
1 MEASURE DRIED
PEPPERMINT LEAVES
~
1/2 MEASURE DRIED
LEMON PEEL
~
1/4 MEASURE
DRIED ROSEMARY
~
1/4 MEASURE
DRIED LAVENDER
~
GLASS JAR AND
CUT-OUT PAPER SCRAPS
~
QUICK-DRYING
ALL-PURPOSE ADHESIVE

ABOVE An all-natural body scrub made with dried flowers and oatmeal makes a luxurious personal gift. The container has been decorated with floral Victorian-style paper cut-outs.

Place all the ingredients in a bowl and mix well together. Now grind small batches of the ingredients in a food processor or coffee mill until you have a coarse powder. Combine the ingredients so they are fully integrated.

Now decorate your jar by gluing a decorative paper cut-out to the outside. You could arrange a border of cut-out shapes round the whole jar or scatter a random pattern of cut-outs all over the surface. When completely finished, and the glue is dry, pour the mixture into the jar.

The scrub can be used on any part of the body, although it is not recommended for the face. To use, dampen the skin. Take a handful of the mixture, add a few drops of water, and rub it briskly over the skin. Rinse off the mixture.

If you use the scrub in the bath, the mixture will make the bath water soft and silky, if a little bit gritty! If you prefer, you can put the mixture into small muslin sachets which can then be moistened and rubbed over the skin or just dropped into the bath to soften the water prior to bathing.

Be sure to write a little label to explain just how best to use the scrub and attach it to the jar or tuck it into the wrapping of the finished gift.

GIFTS FOR GARDENERS

*B*ecause gardeners usually appreciate scented flowers and herbs, they will find scented gifts particularly appealing. Select plants which have fragrant flowers or choose seeds or bulbs which hold the promise of fragrance to come. A keen gardener will usually make space in his or her garden for a special fragrant plant. Other enticing gifts are products made from a harvest of fragrant plants from the garden, such as those using lavender or home-grown aromatic herbs as the main ingredient. You may like to give a collection of items based around one favourite fragrance. Other gifts can be utterly practical, such as soothing hand cream for work-worn hands or anti-insect products.

Package and organise your gifts with common sense. For example, if you are giving bulbs to plant, include a bag of special compost, a decorative pot to put the plants in or a little book on growing bulbs indoors. These sort of collections look lovely packed into a gardening trug or pretty basket which will continue to be useful long after the gifts inside have been depleted. Old or antique baskets often suit the occasion better than very new baskets, and can even be sprayed or colour-washed with paint to harmonise with the gifts inside. Do include instructions on any growing tips for the plants you are giving, or for any of the products that need further explanation.

Lavender Collection

Whether a gardener has rolling acres of land or just a small plot, a lavender collection makes a perfect present. There are several types of lavender from which to choose, and versions with white, pink and various shades of purple flowers. A glossy dark green painted basket makes an ideal container for all the lavender gifts.

1 ROOMY BASKET
~
2 OR 3 DIFFERENT SMALL LAVENDER PLANTS
~
LAVENDER WATER, SEE PAGE 68
~
LAVENDER-COVERED BALLS, SEE PAGE 16
~
DRIED LAVENDER IN BUNCHES
~
RIBBONS IN MAUVE AND PURPLE
~
2 OR 3 SMALL LAVENDER BAGS, SEE PAGE 38
~
LAVENDER CUSHION OR SMALL PILLOW, SEE PAGE 45

Use the recipe on page 68 for lavender water and bottle it into pretty old-fashioned bottles, such as lovely old scent and perfume bottles. Otherwise, use plain medicine-type bottles with simple cork stoppers.

Make the lavender balls from the idea on page 16, using dark purple and highly scented dried flowers. Make small bags and pillows as described on pages 38 and 45 and fill them either with a large scoop of dried lavender flowers or make a more lasting mixture adding ground spices such as cinnamon, cloves, powdered orris root as a fixative and a good dash of lavender essential oil.

Cover the bases of the pots of lavender so no soil spills out and water does not leak.

Take care packing the basket with all the different gifts. You may like to individually wrap the smaller items in mauve tissue paper, but unwrapped gifts in a basket make a spectacular display. Tie a small bunch of dried lavender to the handle of the basket with a pretty piece of gauzy ribbon. To finish, loosely wrap the complete basket in a big swathe of cellophane tied with a bow at the top and attach a label describing the contents.

RIGHT For gardeners who love lavender, choose an assortment of gifts to include in a basket. You may also want to add lavender soap or a sheaf of dried lavender tied with a ribbon.

A Gardener's Basket

~

This basket contains lovely scented plants for a windowsill, conservatory or outdoors in a flower border during the summer season. A bright red-painted basket holds all the gifts, and the colour really sets off the green plants beautifully. Spray paint is the easiest to use on a basket, as it can reach all the awkward places a brush cannot, and it gives an even coating. Car paint is ideal for this project.

1 BASKET, PAINTED RED
~
1 JASMINE PLANT
~
SCENTED PELARGONIUMS
~
SEEDS OF SCENTED PLANTS
~
A COLLECTION OF OLD TERRACOTTA POTS
~
TISSUE PAPER OR BROWN PACKING PAPER
~
PRETTY PLANT LABELS

ABOVE This basket combines lovely decorative plants with practical items, appealing to a gardener's love of beauty and function.

BRIGHT SUEDE AND COTTON GARDENING GLOVES
~
1 BALL GREEN GARDENING TWINE

Re-pot the growing plants into old or interesting containers. Pack the plants into the basket, and tuck the other smaller items around them. Stack the terracotta pots together, and wrap them in tissue or brown paper. Hang the gloves jauntily over the edge of the basket.

Attach a decorative label. You may like to use a picture of a plant or flower cut out from a magazine and glued on to heavy paper or card cut from a postcard. The most suitable images are reproductions from antique herbalist books. Either leave the basket, or over-wrap it with a large piece of cellophane, carefully avoiding squashing the plants. Tie the top of the cellophane with garden twine.

A Herb Basket

This basket for a gardener contains several small living plants and seeds for sowing. Annual herbs are often sold more or less at the seedling stage ready to be potted into larger containers or the garden. Dill, chervil and coriander are herbs which need to be sowed and planted regularly throughout the summer for a constant supply, so they are particularly good herbs to choose. In the spring, choose a generous mixture of different types of annual herbs packed prettily with a flowering plant or two.

SHALLOW NATURAL WILLOW BASKET
~
SELECTION OF ANNUAL AND PERENNIAL HERBS
~
SELECTION OF HERB SEEDS
~
BROWN PAPER AND A LABEL, OPTIONAL

This basket includes a mixture of wild primroses, thyme, chives and French lavender, but you can choose the plants you prefer. Try, however, to include some items which can be appreciated right away, some for a few months ahead and some which should settle down and flourish for years. Take care to ensure that the plants you include will suit the climate, season and soil in which they will be growing.

Include some labels describing the care of the plants. You could also include a book containing herb recipes or on creating a decorative herb garden if the person is a beginner in herb gardening.

Arrange the plants and seed packets in the basket. Wrap the base of the basket in a big sheet of plain brown parcel paper, leaving the top open for the plants to breathe. Tie the whole thing up with string and finish the gift with a brown parcel label.

BELOW A shallow round basket makes an excellent container for pots of growing herbs. The herbs can be planted out in a garden or windowbox or left in their pots to use in the kitchen.

Indoor Herb Pots

Many herbs are suitable for growing indoors, and some will last several months even if you regularly pick leaves for the kitchen. Others make pretty decorative plants which add aroma to the home. Some, like mint, have a natural deterrent effect towards insects, so are doubly useful. Naturally any living plant will need as much light as possible to thrive, without being scorched by direct sunshine or frozen by icy draughts. A windowsill is the usual place for growing herbs, but make sure it provides pleasant, not extreme, conditions.

3 HERB PLANTS
~
3 SMALL TERRACOTTA POTS
~
POTTING COMPOST
~
CONTAINER OR TRAY FOR THE HERB POTS

In this case the herb chosen is rosemary. It has the ability to grow very large, but not if it is confined in small pots indoors. However, keep rosemary plants confined for only several months and then transplant them outside to give them more natural surroundings. While they are indoors, you can snip small pieces off the leaves to use as flavouring in cooking.

There are several varieties of rosemary from which to choose, including tall upright versions and sprawling prostrate ones. The colour of the flowers varies too, from palest mauve to deep blue. Use fairly heavy and gritty compost rather than a very light peat-based compost.

Repot your herbs into terracotta pots, adding more compost as required. Although terracotta pots are prettier than plastic, the plants will require a little more watering. Arrange the pots on a decorative tray, and include a label with instructions on caring for the herb.

BELOW Pots of rosemary make a statuesque and eye-catching arrangement in a sunny window, but they will need to be replanted out of doors or into larger containers as they grow.

Miniature Herb Topiaries

The topiaries are created from cut herbs to look like miniature growing trees clipped into perfect shape. With a lot of time and effort, and more than a little luck, it could be possible to create these pots from real growing plants. You would need to choose your type of plant with care, as many might not be suitable for such a small scale. However, these versions make little green sculptures from thyme and box, and a pair would be a lovely present to give.

FLORISTS' FOAM
~
SMALL TERRACOTTA POT
~
KITCHEN KNIFE OR CRAFT KNIFE
~
SHORT STEMS OF THYME, BOX OR OTHER
FRAGRANT HERBS
~
RIBBON, OPTIONAL

The herbs you choose must have stiffish, woody stems, in order to push the small stalks into the foam. Use a great quantity of herbs. The overall effect should be very dense,

ABOVE A pair of herb topiaries makes a stunning scented arrangement on a mantlepiece, and, with a little skill, they can be made into any shape you desire.

with no hint of spaces or foam showing through. The florists' foam you choose should be quite a bit larger than the size you want your topiary to be; the foam needs to be cut to size and you will need to allow for a margin of error in cutting.

Snip lots of short herb sprigs. Then, soak the block of florists' foam to make it easier to carve. Cut your foam into a sphere, cone or pyramid shape, but also carve a square or round base piece under the shape to push into the terracotta pot. Push the foam into the pot, and make sure the foam shape is upright.

Start to insert the small herb sprigs all over, working round steadily from the base of the florists' foam upwards and round in one direction. When all the foam is completely covered and there are no gaps, trim any wayward pieces with small scissors to achieve a tidy shape. You could decorate the pot with a ribbon, but the topiary is very stylish left completely plain and unadorned.

Gardenia Buttonhole
~

A wonderfully old-fashioned and romantic buttonhole flower can be worn for any formal occasion, and makes a lovely gift for Mother's Day or for a wedding. Gardenias look cool and perfect, as if they were made from porcelain, and their scent is exotic, potent and lasts well. You could also use a camellia or rose to make the same buttonhole decoration.

1 PERFECT FRESH GARDENIA
~
FLORISTS' TAPE
~
SEVERAL GARDENIA LEAVES, EITHER IN A SPRAY OR
SEPARATE BUT EACH WITH SOME STEM
~
WIRE
~
SECATEURS
~
BOX AND TISSUE PAPER, OPTIONAL
~
LONG STRAIGHT PIN

Take care when handling the bloom; once the petals are touched they can turn brown and spoil. The tape is used to bind the stems and their cut ends so that moisture is kept in and the flower and leaves last longer. The old-fashioned

ABOVE A delicate, perfectly formed gardenia makes a romantic-looking buttonhole or a simple corsage, ideal for celebrating special occasions.

tape was like a kind of waxed stretchy paper, but today the tape is a thin, matt, plastic tape, which stretches and grips to itself. It is possible to buy the tape in white, green and brown. The green is natural-looking and makes a less obvious effect than the white.

Hold the gardenia in your hand and bunch the leaves round the bloom as naturally as possible. Wire the stems together to make a tight little spray or posy. Trim the stems at the bottom to all the same length.

Now wrap the tape round the stems. Starting at the top just under the flower, twist the tape down and round the stems, stretching as you go. Enclose the cut edges of the stems with tape at the bottom, and wind the tape back up to the top. You will find it easier to twist the stems rather than the tape.

At the top, cut the tape from the reel and press the end tight against the taped stem; the tape should stay in place. Now place the finished buttonhole in a small box, surrounded by tissue paper or soft packing. Provide a long pin with the buttonhole, to attach the flower to a lapel.

Potted Gardenias

Gardenias are a very special treat to be given. After a period of scarcity on the market, gardenias are being more widely cultivated again and are often sold as small plants producing many flowers. Sometimes they are grown as little standard trees which are particularly beautiful. They have a reputation for being rather difficult to maintain, but they are worth any effort spent. Here a group of small gardenias has been placed into a glazed green pot, which complements their glossy green leaves perfectly.

3-4 SMALL FLOWERING GARDENIAS
~
LARGE POT OR CACHE POT
~
SPECIAL POTTING COMPOST FOR
LIME-HATING HOUSEPLANTS
~
CELLOPHANE AND RIBBON, OPTIONAL

Shake the plants gently from the pots in which they were grown, and arrange them into the new larger pot, filling any gaps with extra soil. Make sure you are not using a soil containing lime, as gardenias cannot tolerate this. Water the gardenias with rain water, if possible, and keep them in a slightly humid atmosphere; gardenias hate conditions which are too hot and drying.

To present the pot as a gift, wrap the plants in a big piece of cellophane, being careful not to crush the blooms, and tie on a bow in a toning colour.

BELOW A green bowl filled compactly with gardenias makes a rounded, full arrangement, perfect for a scented centrepiece.

RIGHT Decorate an assortment of anti-insect lotions and remedies with ribbons and doilies to add a charming touch to a collection of practical gifts.

Anti-insect Kit
~

Gardening outdoors has many benefits, but also a few irritations. Working in the garden on a warm humid evening, if you are unlucky, may bring swarms of midges, mosquitoes or other bothersome insects. However, there are a few natural means of protection, and remedies too if you do not succeed in keeping the insects away. This kit includes a variety of insect repellants and salves, and makes an interesting and unusual gift for someone who spends much time outside, whether gardening, walking or taking exercise.

1 SMALL BASKET
~
QUASSIA CHIPS, AVAILABLE FROM HERBALISTS
~
CITRONELLA ESSENTIAL OIL
~
WITCH HAZEL ESSENTIAL OIL
~
PEPPERMINT ESSENTIAL OIL
~
LEMONGRASS ESSENTIAL OIL
~
LAVENDER ESSENTIAL OIL
~
CHAMOMILE ESSENTIAL OIL
~
DECORATIVE SEALABLE BOTTLES
AND JARS
~
COTTON WOOL AND
A NATURAL SPONGE, OPTIONAL
~
PAPER DOILIES AND BOWS, OPTIONAL

Place 60 ml (4 tablespoons) quassia chips in a bowl. Boil 600 ml (1 pint) water and pour over the quassia chips. Leave the infusion to cool. When cool, strain the liquid, discard the chips, and add a few drops of citronella oil to the liquid. Bottle this to be used on the skin before exposure to humid conditions where there may be a risk of insect bites. Add a pack of the quassia chips and instructions to make more solution and pack these into the basket.

Make up a lotion to pat on to insect bites or stings by mixing 90 ml (6 tablespoons) witch hazel with ten drops of peppermint, lemongrass and lavender essential oil. Pour into tightly stoppered small bottles, label with instructions, and place into the basket.

Also add to the basket small bottles of neat lavender and chamomile essential oils, both of which can be applied directly on to insect bites. In the case of wasp stings, dab the skin first with wine vinegar before applying the essential oils, because the sting should be neutralised before the oil treatment. Also include in the basket cotton wool pads or balls and a small natural sponge.

To make the gift basket look pretty despite its functional purpose, cover the lids of jars or bottles with doily 'hats' and tie a jaunty ribbon bow on the basket handle. Do give detailed instructions on how to use all the gifts you have included in the kit.

Gardener's Hand Cream
~

However careful you are when working in a garden, it is difficult not to remove gloves for some of the jobs which need the attention that only delicate fingers can give. As a result, the ravages of sun and drying winds and the effect of soil and plants can also leave the skin damaged and sore. A soothing healing cream makes a perfect gift for an avid gardener. The cream can also be applied before gardening, inside the gloves, as a preventative measure. Give a small tin or jar of this special mixture along with a new pair of working gloves, and include details on how and when to apply the cream and the ingredients you have used.

30 ML (2 TABLESPOONS) COCOA BUTTER
~
30 ML (2 TABLESPOONS) BLEACHED
BEESWAX GRANULES
~
12 TEASPOONS ALMOND OIL
~
2 CAPSULES VITAMIN E OIL
~
10 DROPS ROSEMARY ESSENTIAL OIL

10 DROPS LAVENDER ESSENTIAL OIL
~
10 DROPS SAGE ESSENTIAL OIL
~
6 DROPS EUCALYPTUS ESSENTIAL OIL
~
SHALLOW WIDE-NECKED JARS OR CONTAINERS
~
BOX AND LABEL, OPTIONAL

Place the cocoa butter and beeswax together in a double-saucepan or in a small bowl over a pan of simmering water. Melt the mixture, stirring constantly.

Warm the almond oil in a separate pan, then slowly pour into the beeswax mixture, beating constantly. Break open the vitamin E capsules and add the contents to the mixture. Stir in thoroughly, then add the drops of essential oils.

When the mixture has cooled, spoon into small jars or suitable containers. Place in a decorative box and label, instructing to store the cream in a cool dark place.

BELOW This hand cream is made from cocoa butter and essential oils to soothe and heal dry, damaged hands. Although ideal for gardeners, the cream is also suitable for anyone whose hands receive rough treatment.

Gift Wrappings

A lovely gift deserves equally lovely presentation. In most cases the wrapping should be simple and not fussy, but it must also be stylish and suitable for the gift inside. Wonderful accessories can be purchased to embellish your gift and add a finishing touch, such as raffia or coloured string, very wide or very narrow ribbons, wire-edged ribbons in a variety of colours and patterns, natural or recycled papers and bows. Sometimes the simplest ideas work best, such as crisp new tissue paper stamped with a smart motif in paint or ink. Cellophane, if it is thick and crackly, can give any present the glamorous touch, while plain old-fashioned brown paper can look as sumptuous as the most expensive gift wraps when teamed with smart labels and thick cotton or paper string.

Spend a little time practising your handwriting for perfectly finished labels and use coloured ink for an extra-special touch. Explore the range of different inks and pens that are available, and find the type that suits your personal style. For example, a gold felt-tip pen gives an elegant touch to a gold-edged tag, or a chunky italic pen looks effective on a brown parcel label. You could also use dry-transfer letters, which are available from stationery shops. These can be rubbed directly on to the label or gift wrap and they give a professionally lettered look.

Covered Boxes

~

Most gifts are best placed in a good solid box which protects the contents. New or second-hand boxes can be covered with fabric or paper for a decorative effect, and the box will look pretty enough to use again. Covering boxes requires a steady hand and the correct tools, but otherwise it is not difficult. Allow yourself a large area of clean space in which to work.

BOXES OF ALL SHAPES
~
FINE-WEAVE COTTON FABRICS, IN COLOURS
OF YOUR CHOICE
~
GIFT WRAPPING OR SUITABLE PAPER
~
FABRIC ADHESIVE
~
PAPER ADHESIVE
~
METAL RULE
~
CRAFT KNIFE
~
SCISSORS
~
DOUBLE-SIDED ADHESIVE
TAPE, OPTIONAL

You will need to take measurements and work according to the size of box you have. If you are using fabric, check that the lid will still fit the box once the box is covered. The easiest method for covering a box is to place your box in the centre of your piece of fabric or paper, wrong-side up. Draw or mark the measurements of the base, then add the measurements of the four sides to create a template. Leave a little extra space around for overlapping.

Cut out your paper or fabric according to the measurements. Glue the base of the box, then place it on the marked base of your covering. Glue a side of the box and smooth the covering over the side, overlapping at the top and corners. Repeat on the other sides, and repeat the whole process for the lid of the box.

Where possible, cut fabric or paper up to edges and overlap only where really necessary. Fabrics can fray, so use your discretion. If you are covering a coloured box, make use of this at the edges, taking your paper or fabric just short of the edge for a neatly defined effect.

RIGHT Choosing your own coloured papers or fabrics for covering boxes makes a truly unique decorative gift box.

Special Paper Wrappings

Some gifts, such as bottles or flat objects, are awkward shapes and wrapping them is a difficult job. Tissue paper is often the most useful type of wrapping, as it can be moulded round almost any shape and the creases that result look interesting rather than crumpled.

HEAVY-WEIGHT PAPER
~
DOUBLE-SIDED TAPE
~
RIBBONS OR STRING
~
SCISSORS
~
THIN CARD, EITHER SMOOTH OR CORRUGATED
~
WRAPPING PAPER OF YOUR CHOICE
~
ADHESIVE
~
METAL RULE
~
CRAFT KNIFE
~
STRING, RIBBONS AND FASTENERS

To make a cylindrical box for a bottle of perfume or wine, wrap heavy-weight, stiff paper round the bottle and fold the bottom edges under, taping very securely. Tie narrow string or ribbon round the top of the bottle and cut the paper above this into deep points, waves or fringes.

Small objects, such as silk scarves, are best packed into flat envelopes, which can be made using various thicknesses of card, either coloured or even corrugated card. Experiment with various envelope shapes, folding edges over and gluing to make pockets. Attach two paper washers with metal fasteners at the point of the envelope lid and on the front of the envelope, and wrap with string to close. Or, add ribbons or strings for fastening. If you are making an envelope from thick hand-made paper, you may like to wrap the whole envelope round with a piece of raffia or twine for a natural-looking wrap.

Small loose gifts, such as hand-made sweets, fit perfectly into paper cones or little bags. Simply roll a sheet of paper or card round into a cone shape and glue along the seam. Bend over the bottom point, and fix this in place at the back, covering it with a small sticky label or decoration if desired. Cut two tiny slots near the top and thread narrow ribbon through to hold the cone. Enclose the sweets or other gift in tissue first to keep it safe inside the cone.

BELOW Here an assortment of paper and card wraps in metallic grey colours are used to enclose awkwardly shaped gifts.

A Gift Hamper
~

A basket hamper is ideal for really special gifts; but unless you can find an old or used hamper, the cost can be fairly expensive. The hamper is a traditional way to present food items, and, filled with a selection of home-made items, would make a lovely gift for someone with a new home. You could adapt the hamper for a hospital present or for a new mother, and the options are endless. This hamper is lined with tissue paper which has been hand-printed with heart motifs.

TISSUE PAPER
~
POTATO, TO MAKE A BLOCK-PRINT STAMP
~
KITCHEN KNIFE
~
WATER-BASED PAINT
~
SMALLER BOXES
~
CURLING PAPER RIBBON
~
1 MEDIUM-SIZED EMPTY WILLOW HAMPER
~
RIBBONS
~
SCENTED PLANTS AND OTHER GIFTS

ABOVE A simple motif, painted on tissue paper and boxes, creates a lovely co-ordinated effect for a selection of gifts in a hamper.

To make the printed tissue, cut a potato in half. Carve a simple motif, such as the heart used here, out of the cut side of one half of the potato. Using water-based paint, brush a little paint on the potato stamp and print on the tissue paper. Repeat the pattern randomly over the tissue paper, or space the motif in uniform lines. Repeat on several sheets of tissue paper and leave to dry. The paper will crackle and wrinkle a little with drying.

Decorate the empty gift boxes with the heart motif, as above. Use the same paint for a matching look. Leave to dry. Insert gifts into the boxes, then tie the boxes with plenty of curled paper ribbon.

Line the basket with the tissue paper, insert the boxes and other gifts, then attach pretty bows to the hamper handle. Transport the hamper with care, leaving the lid open if there are plants inside.

Scented Wrappings
~

If you are giving a scented gift, a lovely idea is to repeat the fragrance on the gift wrap. Unfortunately, essential oils may stain wrapping papers and labels, but an alcohol-based perfume in a spray form can be used to scent paper products as the alcohol will help the perfume evaporate without leaving a mark. Simply spray your gift wrapping paper or tissue papers, labels, ribbons or bows, and leave them to dry before wrapping your gift.

If you are presenting your gift in a card box, simply apply several drops of an essential oil to the inside of the box. The card will absorb the oil and the scent will last for a long time. You may also like to add a few drops of an essential oil to a thin layer of paper wadding or cotton wool. Place the scented papers or cotton wool in the bottom of a gift box, then cover with a piece of gift wrap or tissue paper to hide the wadding. The scent will permeate the box and the gift inside. You could also scent a piece of cotton wool with essential oils, insert it into a tiny envelope or a twist of paper or fabric, and place in the gift box.

To scent ribbons or strings, add a few drops of essential oil or a little perfume to a small quantity of water. Always test with your nose, adding more perfume or essential oil as necessary. Soak the ribbons and strings for several hours, then leave them to dry before tying them on to your gift.

Of course, the most attractive way to add scent to gifts is to tie on a scented decoration, such as a tiny stem or two of dried flowers. If the scent of the dried flowers is not strong enough, add a few drops of essential oil, matching the scent to the flowers.

Ribbons and Bows
~

Although ribbons and bows may seem such small details, they are really the focal point of the gift wrap and the means by which the gift is opened. Avoid tying elaborate knots or making the fastenings so complicated that the ribbon can not be undone and used again.

A range of beautiful ribbons is available from gift shops and department stores. Choose some of the more unusual ribbons and bows, such as velvet, taffeta, satin (single- and double-faced), wire-edged, organdie, pleated and picot-edged, to name just a few. Ribbons are available in an assort-ment of widths, from the narrowest gauge to great wide sashes. Not only is there a rainbow choice of colours, but also different designs too, such as spots, florals, stripes and checks. Avoid the cheapest ribbons, such as those sold for floral work, as they are likely to fray and crumple, and use real fabric ribbons whenever possible.

Wire-edging means that making beautiful bows is simple. The bows can be 'tweaked' into position and retain their shape. Special ribbons made from polyester, paper or plastic can be made to curl when run hard against a flat edge of a metal rule or the blades of a scissors. These ribbon curls are fun to make and inexpensive, so you can be really generous and create a frivolous look. Explore dress-making departments of shops to find interesting and unusual bindings and edgings which can be used instead of ribbon. Wonderful linen weaves and plain cotton tapes, for example, look stylish and smart and are usually inexpensive compared with ribbons from a reel.

Knitting yarns also make great economical ribbons. Fancy chenilles and bouclees are available in a large hank or ball, and can be used really lavishly. You can also plait and twist yarns together to make thicker ropes or multi-coloured versions for different effects.

BELOW Choose ribbons, bows and decorations for your gift with care, co-ordinating colours and images for the most striking effect.

LEFT Plain labels can be decorated with gold glitter stars and gold cord, as here, or with any other motifs you desire. Keep a supply of plain labels on hand for adapting to your specific needs.

Labels and Tags

Labels and tags are both decorative and informative. They can hold a personal message from the giver or offer added information about the gift inside. However, you will probably like to include a more informative label inside the packaging so you do not spoil the surprise. When especially decorative and attached directly to the gift with ribbon, labels are perfectly suitable as the only gift wrapping.

You do not have to use ready-made labels, especially if you have gone to the trouble of making or finding unusual wrappings. A good way of producing your own rather special labels is to adapt very simple parcel or luggage tags. You may like to attach a small stick-on gold glitter star to the plain tag, or just replace the small piece of string in the label with a piece of gold cord or beautiful fine ribbon.

Sealing wax can also be used on labels by melting a small amount on to the plain card, then pressing a special print block into the warm wax to create a detailed motif. Small pieces of lace, paper motifs, cut-outs or confetti can also

be glued on to a plain label to create a decorative design.

A small dried flower or even a single dried flower petal can be glued to a plain tag. You may like to add a drop of an essential oil to the petal for a scented label. Dried leaves can be gilded and glued in place or you can buy small gold paper leaves from cake decorating suppliers which can be glued in place; do use gold inks or felt-tip pens for your message to co-ordinate with the gold leaves.

If your wrapping paper is beautiful and elaborate, then cut a small piece from another sheet and glue the wrapping paper to a small piece of card. If the design is floral, then cut around a leaf or flower shape. Punch a hole in the card, and thread with ribbon. Tie this to the ribbon-wrapped parcel.

When you see suitable ingredients for your own labels, buy them and set them aside, so you always have a supply of materials. You can also recycle images from other items, and you may like to cut out images from greeting cards, post cards or photographs. Collecting different images and motifs from a variety of sources will enable you to create an interesting and unusual label whenever you need one.

DIAGRAMS AND PATTERNS

The Roll
~
(page 40)

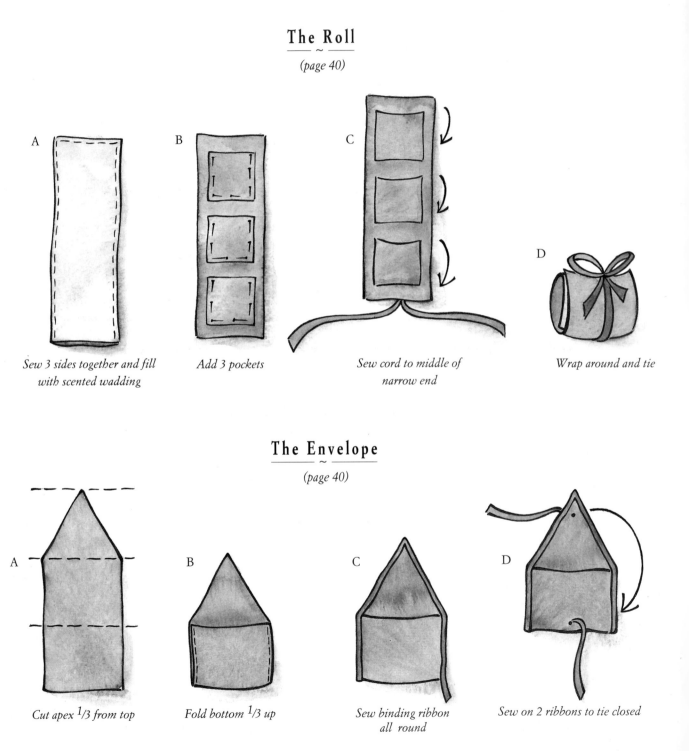

A

Sew 3 sides together and fill with scented wadding

B

Add 3 pockets

C

Sew cord to middle of narrow end

D

Wrap around and tie

The Envelope
~
(page 40)

A

Cut apex 1/3 from top

B

Fold bottom 1/3 up

C

Sew binding ribbon all round

D

Sew on 2 ribbons to tie closed

Folded Wallet

~

(page 41)

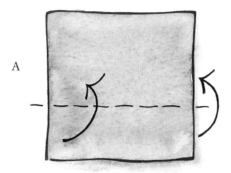

A

Fold edge up 10cm (4in) to form large pocket

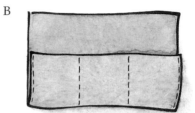

B

Divide into 3 small pockets

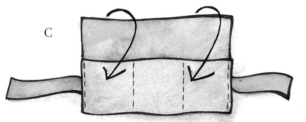

C

Fold remaining flap over. Sew ribbon round

D

Fold in half and tie closed

Satin Drawstring Bag

~

(page 41)

A

Sew down sides
leaving a small gap

B

Cut circle of satin for base

C

Make channel for
drawstring

D

Thread through ribbon
and tie together

GLOSSARY OF ESSENTIAL OILS

Below are listed some of the essential oils available from herbalists, with a brief description of their scent and their properties. A good herbalist will have further information on the uses of these and other essential oils.

BASIL A sweet and spicy scented oil, basil has a calming, uplifting effect and helps alleviate fatigue and insomnia.

BENZOIN Benzoin is an antiseptic oil with a relaxing and warming effect. It helps rid the skin of impurities.

BERGAMOT With a sweet and fruity scent and refreshing properties, bergamot oil is excellent in a bath, as a massage oil, or in pot-pourris and sweet powders.

BLACK PEPPER With a woody and spicy scent, black pepper oil has stimulating and warming properties, and is particularly useful for relieving muscular aches.

CARDAMOM Cardamom oil has a warm and spicy aroma, and is often used in India in perfumes and incenses. The oil is refreshing and invigorating, and useful in baths or bath products.

CARROT SEED This sweet and earthy scented oil is helpful for dry skin conditions and it is thought to help restore the skin's elasticity.

CEDARWOOD A balsamic-woody scented oil, cedarwood oil has calming properties, and it is useful for oily skin and hair, and as an antiseptic and insect-repellant.

CHAMOMILE A deep blue-coloured oil, with calming and soothing properties, chamomile is particularly useful for insomnia and skin irritations.

CINNAMON With a warm, sweet and spicy scent, cinnamon oil is known for its invigorating properties. It must be heavily diluted before using.

CLARY SAGE A spicy and floral scented oil, clary sage oil soothes and relaxes.

CLOVE Clove oil has a woody and spicy scent and stimulating properties.

CYPRESS Cypress oil has a sweet pine scent and astringent properties, and helps varicose veins and broken capillaries.

EUCALYPTUS An oil with a strong medicinal scent, eucalyptus oil is useful for relieving cold symptoms and sinus conditions. It is stimulating, an antiseptic, and an insect repellant.

EUCALYPTUS CITRIADORA With a fresh lemony scent, eucalyptus citriadora oil has refreshing and astringent properties.

FENNEL Fennel oil has a sweet fresh scent with aniseed undertones.

GERANIUM An oil with a highly floral and green aroma, geranium oil is useful for treating anxiety and dry skin. It is particularly useful in baths, massage oils and skin creams, and as an insect repellant and refreshing astringent.

GINGER With a warm, fresh and spicy scent, this oil is popular in perfume blends. It is a stimulating oil, suitable for baths and bath products.

GRAPEFRUIT Grapefruit oil is citrus-scented and has astringent properties.

JASMINE With a highly floral and exotic scent, this oil is perfect for perfumes. It also helps dry skin conditions.

JUNIPER Juniper oil helps oily skin and is excellent for a refreshing bath to stimulate circulation.

LAVENDER Sweet-smelling and antiseptic, lavender oil is useful for inflamations of the skin, burns, wounds and bites, as well as in a massage oil or bath. Lavender is also helpful for treating insomnia.

LEMON With its sweet lemon scent, lemon oil is often used in perfumes for its fruity note. It is also an antiseptic and astringent for the skin, and helpful for insect bites.

LEMONGRASS An oil with a grassy lemon scent, lemongrass oil helps problem skins and is useful as an insect repellant.

LIME With a sharp lime scent, lime oil is an astringent, useful for oily skin.

MARJORAM An oil with a sweet herbal scent, marjoram has relaxing properties and is useful to relieve stress, anxiety and insomnia.

MELISSA (LEMON BALM) A sweet-scented oil, melissa oil is calming and uplifting, and useful to ease tension and stress headaches.

NEROLI With a highly floral scent, neroli oil is used in eau de cologne. It has relaxing properties, and is useful to ease anxiety and insomnia, as well as to soothe dry skin.

ORANGE Orange oil is a fruity-smelling oil with a refreshing effect.

PATCHOULI With a dry, woody smell, patchouli is used as a fixative in perfumes. As an astringent oil it helps treat problem skin and oily scalps. The oil is also excellent for dry skins and is said to have cell-regenerating properties.

PEPPERMINT Peppermint oil is minty-scented and has a cooling and refreshing effect on the skin.

PETIGRAINE With its sweet floral smell, similar to neroli, petigraine oil is excellent for refreshing massage blends or bath oils.

ROSE A sweet floral-scented oil, rose oil is traditionally used for perfumes. It has a relaxing effect and benefits dry, sensitive skins.

ROSE GERANIUM Often used as a substitute for the similar but more expensive rose oil.

ROSEMARY With a herbaceous scent and stimulating properties, rosemary oil helps the hair and scalp.

SAGE An herbaceous-scented oil, sage oil is useful in baths or in massage oils to relieve aches and pains.

SANDALWOOD With its balsamic, woody scent, sandalwood oil makes an excellent massage oil for men and helps dry, itchy skin.

THYME Thyme oil is a stimulating oil useful in baths to ease aches and pains and to invigorate.

YLANG YLANG With an exotic floral scent, ylang ylang is used in perfumes. It also has a relaxing, sedative effect.

INDEX